The MIKE SCHMIDT STUDY

Hitting Theory,
Skills and Technique

The MIKE SCHMIDT STUDY

Hitting Theory, Skills and Technique

Mike Schmidt
& Rob Ellis

McGriff & Bell Inc.
Atlanta, GA 30324

The Mike Schmidt Study: Hitting Theory, Skills and Technique
by Mike Schmidt and Rob Ellis. © 1994 by Rob Ellis and
published by: McGriff & Bell Inc., 1579 F Monroe Drive N.E.,
Suite 134, Atlanta, Georgia 30324. All rights reserved.

- Historical photographs: National Baseball Library, Cooperstown, N.Y.
- Modern player photographs: R & R Sports Group, Staten Island, N.Y.
- Youth shots: Diane Haddad
- Sequence shots: Mountain Lion Books/Jon Naso
- Artwork: Louise Bauer
           Paul Cheney
           Robert Cupp
           Art Jacobs
           Susan Seavitt
- Cover and book design: Alan G. Hartman

Library of Congress Catalog Card No. 93-77354

ISBN 0-9634-6092-7 (pbk.)
ISBN 0-9634-6091-9 (hdbk.)

1 2 3 4 5 Printing/Year 97 96 95 94 93

Printed in the United States of America

Dedication

To ballplayers and coaches who are
striving to excel at the game they love.

Contents

Foreword

America has been fascinated by the game of baseball for more than 150 years, long enough for it to be crowned our National Pastime. And for most observers, the focal point of this fascination has been on the man holding the bat. Hitting is the most sacred of all our sports skills, and it may be the most mysterious. Yet since the game began there has never been a comprehensive analysis, an exegesis, of what has alternately fascinated and baffled man since the game began in 1836. Never have we enjoyed a comprehensive study. No one has ever shown why one hitter excels and another fails. Why one man will hit .240 and another man .340. Without this information no one can tell the .240 hitter what to do to hit .340. That is the goal of this book: to reveal the techniques and skills of successful hitting in clear, simple terms. I hope it will uncomplicate things: lay bare the facts about hitting; remove some of the bewilderment surrounding such a precious skill; and increase the fascination.

Before the late 1970s, the hitter's "Bible" was *The Science of Hitting* by Ted Williams, and his method became known as the Rotation System. The late Charlie Lau came on the scene and, along with the success of his prize pupil George Brett, embellished the old Weight Shift Hitting System. With this, Lau became the hitting master of the late 70s and 80s. The weight shift "torch" has now been passed to Walt Hriniak, who is adding touches of his own. All of these men have made large contributions. I know their theories well. But I am aware of another way to hit, because after I had gone through both styles, I subscribed to neither Williams' or Lau's system in its entirety. I, and other accomplished hitters, combined elements of both systems into something different, something as successful or even more so. It is this Combined System of hitting, a Rotation-Weight Shift System, I want to explain.

My hitting career was filled with experimentation. I tinkered with my swing maybe more than any successful hitter in baseball history, and I feel it paid off. My "role" models were Dick Allen, Hank Aaron, and Roberto Clemente. From Allen I got the "down" swing, from Aaron wrists and high hands, from Clemente use of my entire body and, finally, hitting to all fields. With these great hitters serving as my models, I added my own natural ability, a desire to be the best, and a solid mental game to become a very successful major league hitter. If only I could have had Pete Rose's intensity I'd have played three more years and gotten 3,000 hits!

As I look back, I would say my most important gift was "feel." I could always feel a good swing and log it into memory, or alter it slightly with what I'd learned from trial-and-error, and adjust from bad to good remarkably fast. I believe this ability came from plain swinging the bat continuously over many, many years. It's the combination of this feel, the experimentation and tinkering, and an infinite number of hours spent discussing hitting with everyone from Rose to Williams that inspired me to compile *The Mike Schmidt Study*. I hope that these gifts will allow me to be a helpful hitting coach for you.

MIKE SCHMIDT

I've known Mike Schmidt since 1969, when we played against each other in the summer Central Illinois Collegiate League. We've crossed paths many times since then. When Mike mentioned the idea of this hitting book in casual conversation, I was quite interested. I knew what kind of a hitter he was in college, and also what a great hitter he had become in the majors. To be honest, there was a gap in his success from college to Hall of Fame status. Not many doubted he would make it, but not many were ready to think he'd be the kind of hitter to hit over 500 home runs and win several MVP trophies. What linked his college career to the Hall of Fame was the amount of work, dedication, and mental toil he put in. But few Hall of Famers are willing to take the same time and effort to get those ideas into print. They don't want to roll up their sleeves and work on a book like they did their baseball skills. But when Mike mentioned that he'd like to get what he learned on paper, really get into it, I caught a fever. Maybe here, I thought, was the Hall of Famer willing to dedicate himself to sharing the depth of his knowledge. Mike said he'd made some discoveries during his career, and he believed that together they might constitute a new theory. Perhaps it could be a Third Force, Williams being the first, Lau the second. I offered to help him write it down. He said it wasn't just another hitting book he wanted, but an exegesis. He sounded as if he wanted to go from A to Z and not miss a letter, covering anything and everything pertinent to the study of hitting. And he felt he was the person to try.

I didn't doubt him. Mike said he wanted a book with all the hitting systems represented. He wanted everything from how Ty Cobb hit to how he (Mike) hit, with Williams and Lau in between. He wanted to add to these men's ideas, and if together it made a new theory, then the time had come to get it out. He wanted a true study. What impressed me was his yearning for comprehensiveness. As he was talking, I think he was thinking of himself as a younger player, and that he knew there were other young players as hungry as he had been. I, too, was once a hungry young ballplayer. And so we decided to begin.

Like any writer, I am a bit perfectionistic. What I write must be sound, particularly in a hitting book which will be read by a lot of kids looking for help. And I have some unalterable ideas about hitting which were proven to me by my own major league experience. Luckily, Mike and I thought alike in a lot of disputable matters concerning hand action, swing planes, weight shift, etc. That is not to say we didn't have some differences of opinion, but where we butted heads we brought in the opinions of a dozen other experts. As a general rule I deferred to Mike, who took the job of weighing their opinions and declaring a final word. In this regard, when the pronoun "I" is used, this denotes Mike.

Both Mike and I, two picky guys when it comes to hitting, are pleased with this study. It is our shared hope that we bring to players, coaches, and hitting *aficionados* alike, the closest thing to the final word in hitting to date. I believe it is.

ROB ELLIS

Introduction

This book is divided into two sections. Part One is an examination of the existing hitting systems and their underlying physical mechanics and principles. It is intended for coaches, *advanced* players of professional caliber, and hitting enthusiasts who want to study and pass on knowledge to younger players, and fathers who want to teach their sons. Throughout the book we compare the acquisition of hitting skills to the building of a house. In this analogy, the coach is the on-site builder and the hitters are the skilled laborers. The coach should be the holder of the blueprint (Part One) while the hitters concern themselves with the nuts and bolts of house construction (Part Two).

Part Two deals with the Combined Hitting System lessons for the player. These lessons direct the player's natural style into an effective hitting approach sufficient to succeed at any level of play. The goal of this book is not the re-creation or reconstruction of a hitter's style. It is to lay a skillful foundation and enhance the hitter's natural style via major league knowledge.

Naturally, the coach has business in both Part One and Part Two. The player's focus should be centered on Part Two, although he should carefully study Chapter 5, "The Combined Hitting System", which is the sum of my personal hitting approach.

The reader should proceed slowly in some sections of this book. Do not be discouraged from re-reading many sections. *Teaching* consists of explaining the same thing over many times, and *learning* consists of hearing the same thing again and again. You'll need to re-read *and* re-think. If this discourages you, I'm afraid you're not ready to learn. When going through the lessons in Part Two, we suggest you study, understand, and demonstrate the skills in each lesson before proceeding to the next one. This will allow the proper sequence. When the lessons are finished this way they can serve as a reference.

To get the most out of this book, get out of your chair periodically with a bat in your hands and go through the movements described. Translate the words into feeling and action. Mimic the pictures. Have faith in our wisdom and become your own coach.

Preface

Make no mistake about it: men compete *with their minds*, not their brute force and physical talents alone. The *smarter* man will ultimately win the day.

That is why this book was written. Within its pages lies much new knowledge for every coach and hitter, from Will Clark, big league slugger, to Tony Jones or Chris Gibson, high school hopefuls. If you can read, you can become a better hitter.

No two hitters are alike, nor should they be. Different skeletal structures, bone lengths, muscle placements and strengths, require diversity. But every hitter, regardless of his physical differences, can move and *place himself in action* using successful techniques. Example: every hitter can hold the bat away from or close to his body, raise it or lower it, albeit at slightly different lengths. All hitters can lift their leg to stride, regardless of leg length. *So movement and action can be prescribed.* Through repetition this movement and action can become *acquired* and *natural*, and the hitter can have complete control over the type of hitter he will become. Any movement Boggs or Clark makes can be effectively duplicated. The key is repetition. Call it what you will—practice, rehearsal, mimicry, or an impression—*repetition* is the key to acquiring new movement.

Neurophysiology shows that muscle memory is identical to mind memory. Read the Gettysburg address ten times and you won't have it memorized. Ten more times will give your memory a few phrases, maybe some sentences. Read it over 500 times *aloud* and you will have it memorized. Keep reading it and you will be able to add pause, emphasis, drama, feeling. You will be able to choreograph gestures. Keep working and you might become as convincing as Abraham Lincoln.

Perform a physical movement in a similar sequence and the same phenomenon will occur. You will become comfortable with the new movement. Just don't think twenty or fifty times will do it. Think in terms of hundreds and thousands of repetitions. It was the great Rogers Hornsby, a lifetime .358 hitter from the right side, who said, "A great hitter isn't born, he's made. He's made out of practice, fault correction, and confidence."

Without further delay, let us embark on learning the most heralded skill in sports, hitting a pitched baseball.

Five Hitting Principles

Much of the discussion on hitting systems revolves around five basic hitting principles. Understanding these five principles from an anatomical and physical standpoint is necessary to this study.

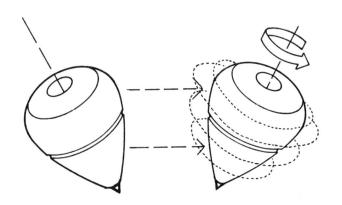

1. "Weight Shift" versus Hip Rotation

"Weight shift" is the forward shift of the body's center of gravity from the back leg to the front leg. Weight shift is a linear, forward, one-dimensional movement.

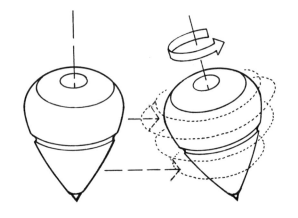

Hip rotation action of the pelvic structure is circular and results from both legs pushing on the hip structure from two opposing directions.

All hitting systems use both circular hip rotation and linear weight shift, although their uses are in different proportions. The "Weight Shift System" emphasizes linear movement, the "Rotation System" emphasizes rotational movement. Combining the power of both movements results in increased energy, comprising a "Combined Hitting System."

2. Rear Arm versus Front Arm

When positioned in the batting stance, the rear arm (also called top hand when referring to hand action), due to its anatomical angle from the shoulder, and the position of muscle insertions and attachments of the triceps and deltoid, is positioned more favorably to exert force in a forward direction than is the front arm. Also, the position of the rear arm (top hand) on the bat is closer to the midpoint, the bat's center of gravity. From a physical law standpoint, in addition to its anatomical advantages, this rear arm is in a position to impart more strength to the bat than the front arm (bottom hand).

One way you can feel this comparison is to swing the bat one-handed, giving each arm a separate chance. If you do, you will see that when the rear arm swings the bat, the hips are able to rotate smoothly, fully. From the picture, see how proper rear arm action effectively turns the hips. Also, notice also how easily the shoulders can rotate on a level plane. The result is a smooth, level swing.

But when the front arm swings the bat, the front shoulder has to fly open in an effort to add force, because the front arm is weaker. Notice the uneven, upward rotation of the shoulders compared to the top hand picture. The shoulders are forced to compensate by pushing backwards on the hip structure, stopping hip and shoulder rotation. This way, the force of the front shoulder must push against the opening action of the hip structure to do its work. Using only the front arm to swing makes the body look like it has gone into shock from the effort.

Thus, from a physical law standpoint, the position of the rear arm allows it to impart greater force in moving the bat. This is clearly seen when we get behind and push a stalled car rather than hook our arm around a bumper to pull it. Anatomically, the triceps and shoulder muscles are positioned to impart greater force *pressing* forward than in *pulling* forward. This explains why we use the force of the back arm in putting shots, throwing, striking a punching bag, or anything else which requires force.

The front arm, or bottom hand, is closest to the target of the swing. This puts it in a favorable position to lead the bat accurately and determine its direction. The rule might be this: for accuracy (golf, Weight Shift System hitting)

Rear Arm

Front Arm

front arm dominance. For power (Rotation System Hitting, track field events, boxing) rear arm dominance.

Richie Zisk: "I think the swing is comprised of two parts. The bottom arm acts as kind of a guide to put the bat in position to use the top hand. Once this happens, the bat is thrown or pushed into the ball by the top hand."

Frank Robinson says the same thing a bit more concisely: "The top hand finishes off what the bottom hand starts."

I always wanted to hit the ball with back spin because this would get it through the infield quicker, and it would carry further in the air. The top hand force is what gives the back spin to the ball, which allows it to carry farther.

3. The Law of Conservation of Angular Momentum

The Law of Conservation of Angular Momentum dictates that limbs (arms or legs) positioned *away* from a rotating axis drain energy from that axis and *slow down* the rotation.

This law can be seen operating in the spins of the figure skater. The figure skater goes into the spin with his arms and a leg outstretched. When he pulls them in close to his body (center of gravity), the tremendous rotation results. When the figure skater wishes to slow down or stop, he puts his arms out once again to drain off the rotation energy. Apply this principle to hitting: when the bat is held closer to the body in the stance, the trunk can spin quicker and the bat moves faster.

4. Bat Angle

Any bat held vertically in the stance (straight up and down) will initiate a long loop in its path to the ball, using valuable time. Worse, gravity acts to pull the head of the vertical bat down below the hands during the swing, which nullifies top hand action and hinders hip rotation. The swing becomes warped into an uppercut.

A bat which is held more horizontally in the stance, at a forty-five degree angle or flatter, will have greater efficiency to the strike zone. Less time will be required getting it to the point of contact. More, the effect of gravity is minimized so top hand action and hip rotation are complete. Also, the path of the bat is straight and level.

From the vertical bat position gravity pulls the head of the bat into a loop and the front shoulder pulls the arms up to their level.

A few great hitters started with a vertical (straight up) bat angle, and if it feels right for you, try it. Just remember that a level swing cannot come out of a vertical bat angle. The flatter the bat angle, the shorter and quicker the stroke.

5. Level Swing Production

Horizontal bat angle.

The best hitter, from a personal and team standpoint, is the one who consistently swings at the ball on a level plane in the effort to produce line drives. It's not just the line drive that makes the hitter productive, but when he "mis-hits" the ball, which will happen over 50% of his at-bats, he hits hard ground balls rather than fly balls. *Balls hit in the air are a waste. Ninety-five percent of fly balls are certain outs.* Ground balls get through the infield for hits, move the runners up, and put pressure on infielders. *They are always potentially productive.* More runs are knocked in with ground balls than fly balls.

This may come as a surprise from a home run hitter, but that is how strongly I believe in the level stroke. Many, many of my home runs were hit with a level cut, which produced backspin on the ball for distance. My best years at the plate, those combining my top average with home run production, came after I discovered my true level cut. My true level cut felt like I was swinging *down*, but films showed it to be level, on a direct collision course with the pitch.

I'll tell you more about my true level cut later. Right now let's study a bit of hitting history.

BALL TRAJECTORY vs. PRODUCTIVITY

Key:	S	=	Strike
	O	=	Out
	P	=	Productive
	PP	=	Potentially Productive

Solid and mis-hit contact hit potential.

Part One: Hitting Theory

Chapter 1
The Evolution of Hitting

Every batter needs to adopt a style consistent with his physical size, speed, strength, and coordination. To thoroughly understand hitting, and choose the proper mechanical action to use, you must examine current hitting theory and principles. By dissecting the existing theories we are not advocating a particular style in its entirety, but we do so as a means of conveying hitting principles.

At this point in hitting history, two complete hitting systems have evolved from one prototype. Many combinations of these hitting systems are in use, but to understand hitting these two systems serve quite well, particularly because they lie on different ends of the hitting spectrum in terms of purpose and physical action. When you read Chapter 5 you will see that my beliefs about hitting place me between Lau and Williams.

Hitting Theories and Their Proponents

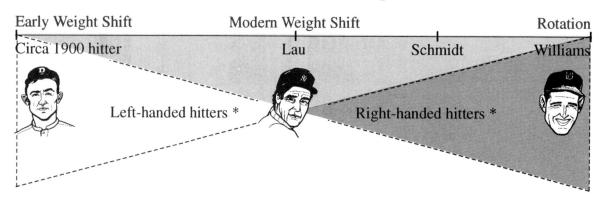

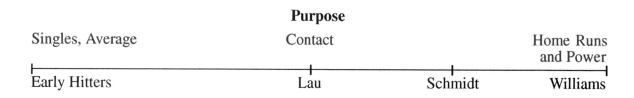

---

* Left-and right-handed hitters evolve into different hitting styles. See chapter 6: Left-handed Hitting versus Right-handed Hitting.

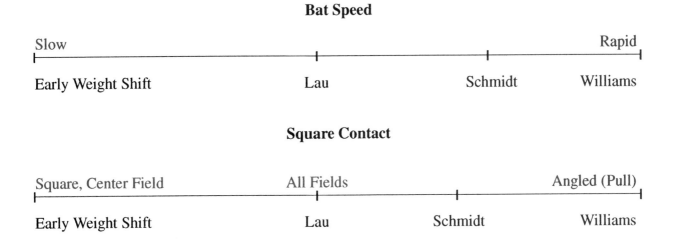

Bat Speed

Slow   Rapid

Early Weight Shift   Lau   Schmidt   Williams

Square Contact

Square, Center Field   All Fields   Angled (Pull)

Early Weight Shift   Lau   Schmidt   Williams

In the table below, note the progressive features as the emphasis goes from mere contact (Early Weight Shift System) to power production (Rotation System). On examination of these hitting systems, many body placements and subsequent actions are *opposite* each other.

Feature	Weight Shift (Pure)	Lau Weight Shift	Rotation
Proponent	early hitters	Lau, Hriniak	Williams
Hand placement	out/low	medium to high	low, close
Foot placement	even	even	even/open
Hip rotation	restricted	approaching but < 90°	90° (full) plus
Plane of swing	level	level	uppercut
Bat angle	flat	45 to 90 degrees	vertical
Stride	long	medium to long	short to medium
Head movement	maximum	moderate	minimum
Dominant hand	bottom	bottom	top
Jump to first	excellent	medium	poor
Conducive to	left-handed	both*	RH/LH power
"Contact"	square	all fields	angled (pull)
Bat speed	slow	medium to rapid	rapid
Purpose	batting average	batting average	power
Arm action	pull w/front side	pull w/front arm	hammering top hand
Description	yank	glide	push
Bat weight	heavy	light/medium	light
* With an edge to the left-handed hitter.			

About the only similarities these styles share is that they start in a stance and end in a follow-through. Ideally, with the understanding of the two theories—Weight Shift and Rotation—a selection of mechanics can be tailored to the individual hitter as it relates to desired purpose, physical characteristics, or batting problems.

Johnny Evers.

Ty Cobb.

Chapter 2
The Early Weight Shift System, Circa 1900

A historical look at early hitting style (circa 1900) is valuable in its relation to developing the modern hitting systems of Lau and Williams.

It is fitting to begin with the Weight Shift System because it is the oldest hitting system that exists. Indeed, in its pure form, the Weight Shift System is an ancient one, with its roots buried deep in the dead ball era. Ty Cobb was a wonderful weight shift hitter, as were such notables as Paul Waner, Harry Walker, Matty Alou, Al Oliver, and Roberto Clemente, where emphasis was on back-to-front momentum of the hitter. Basic elements of the early weight shift style were passed on over the years by hitting instructors like Waner, Walker, and Wally Moses (all left-handed hitters) into the modern era. Walker dusted the system off some, and subsequently Lau updated the system by emphasizing existing features and adding some new emphasis until he had created a newer, modernized version. But in its pure form, the Weight Shift System began in the days of the heavy hickory bats, bats so heavy the hitter had to throw his weight forward to lug, or carry, the heavy bat through the strike zone.

Prior to 1910, the hitter's energy was spent pulling the bat through with outstretched arms, which left little opportunity for hip rotation. The Early Weight Shift hitter escorted the bat through with his forward momentum.

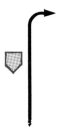

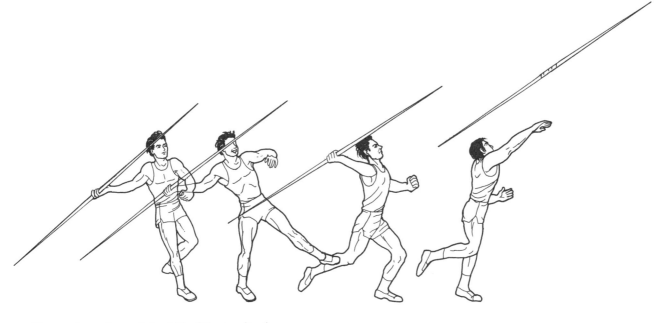

Forward running weight shift of the javelin thrower.

When comparing the Weight Shift System to the newer style of hitting—the Rotation System—it is best to hold in mind two athletes: the javelin thrower and the shot putter. The javelin thrower principally uses forward momentum to develop his power, much like the early weight shift hitter. The shot putter, working in a small circumference, is like the rotation hitter, using body rotation to develop his power and thrust.

Hallmarks of the Early Weight Shift System: **1)** weight transfer from back leg over front leg; **2)** elongated arc; **3)** level plane of swing; **4)** restricted hip rotation because of the exaggerated forward lunge.

Stance

In the Dead Ball era there was no advantage in pulling the ball or hitting it in front of home plate. The Early Weight Shift hitter strove for square contact over the plate, so his stance was located a good distance away from the plate. Often his feet began close together in preparation for a long forward stride to generate forward momentum. Often the bat was held low for maximum pull upward and forward by the shoulders.

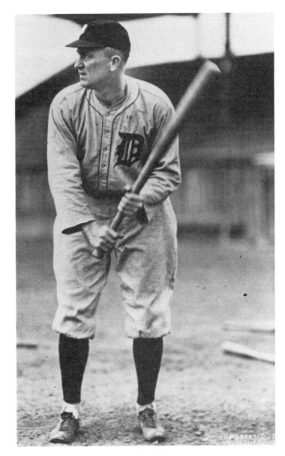

Ty Cobb in early weight shift stance.

Ty Cobb. Notice the bat is pulled through with low, outstreatched arms.

Mechanical Movement

From this stance the action begins. The body simply "slides" forward from the stance into the swing. To do this, the hitter pushes off his back foot into the stride. This is the beginning of the weight shift. Weight is thrown forward by the rear leg onto the front leg, so that the weight goes from back to front. The center of gravity moves in a straight line toward the pitcher. That is the totality of any weight shift—weight goes from back leg to front leg in the stride.

With the forward momentum, the arms begin pulling the bat through the strike zone. This "pulling" action of the arms tends toward *front arm dominance.* The whole front side pulls the bat forward on a level path to the contact area.

The most notable aspect of the Early Weight Shift is that the weight shift keeps going *over* the front leg. Note that the front leg does not offer pronounced resistance to the weight shift (see Baker). If it did, sudden hip rotation would occur, something of no importance to the Early Weight Shift hitter because contact, not power, was his goal. During the weight shift the front leg takes the weight, *it does not fight against the weight transfer.*

"Home Run" Baker taking the weight shift over bent front leg.

The follow-through of the weight shift hitter minimized body rotation and emphasized forward momentum for a good jump out of the box. (With the dead ball, leg hits were at a premium.) The torso remained partially rotated over the front leg while the front shoulder brought the bat around.

"Home Run" Baker in early weight shift follow-through over bent front leg.

It is useful to note here that by pulling the bat through with forward momentum, the front arm extends toward the pitcher and *delays the arced follow through of the bat*. This gives the bat an *elongated, flat arc*. The elongated arc allows the bat to remain in the strike zone *for a longer period of time*, allowing for more square contact.

It is interesting to follow the sequencing action of the weight shift because it lays bare the purpose of the Weight Shift System, which is *batting average and contact* rather than bat speed and power. In the dead ball era, there was no sense going for distance. The Early Weight Shift hitting system was a singles hitting system, a system geared for batting average and not

Elongated arc of early weight shift swing.

power. "Base hit" contact was meant to take place over the plate, and by leaving the bat in the strike zone longer with an elongated arc, more contact could be gained.

It should be noted that if the Weight Shift System gives dominance to the front arm and front side in lugging the bat forward (often with extended arms), this negates the contribution of the stronger rear arm.

A working knowledge of the Weight Shift System, and particularly the principles of the mechanics it employs, can go a long way in selection of proper mechanics. The hitter can employ one or more of its movements to remedy problems created by a bat that is moving too fast.

Advantages of the Early Weight Shift System

1. With the level swing, the hitter will get more contract, more square, center field contact, although the contact may be "dull" because of the slightly decreased bat speed. He'll get hit on the label and end of the bat more often, due to the slower bat speed. But more contact means more hits, fewer strikeouts, and a higher batting average.

2. The hitter will get a great jump out of the batter's box, which translates into more leg hits. The weight shift can be converted into the first stride toward first base simply by bending the knee and continuing the forward momentum.

3. The weight shift hitter is most effective on the pitch from the middle of the plate to the outside corner. The pitch away from the hitter gives him more distance to work with, which means he has more time. The slightly slower bat characteristics of the weight shift system are perfectly conducive to hitting the pitch on the outside half of the plate.

4. Because of the slow bat characteristics of the Early Weight Shift System, the level swing, and the great jump out of the box, it is most conducive to *left-handed hitting*. This will be covered further in Chapter 6, "Stroke Adaptions: Left-handed Hitting Versus Right-handed Hitting."

Disadvantages of the Early Weight Shift System

1. Exaggerated forward head movement. During his stride, the weight shift hitter travels forward as much as four feet at approximately walking speed, two to four miles-per-hour. With the eyes traveling forward, and the pitch speeding toward them, the velocities can be added. When the pitcher throws 85 miles-per-hour, the weight shift hitter's eyes can be seeing 87-89 miles-per-hour.

2. Power is sacrificed for contact. Loss of hip rotation and the "snap" extension from the top hand restricts long ball potential.

3. The weight shift hitter, because of the inhibited rotation of the hips and secondary role of the top hand, is vulnerable to pitches on the inside half of the plate.

4. Balance can be a problem to the weight shift hitter. His only option to employ more power is to thrust the weight more violently off the back foot onto the front foot. A lunge, or forward loss of balance, can result if the stride is taken too forcefully.

5. Because of the delayed rotation of the hips and secondary role of the top hand, which compromises bat speed, the weight shift style of hitting is less conducive to right-handed hitting. (See Chapter 6, "Left-handed Hitting versus Right-handed Hitting".)

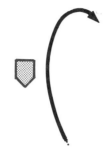

Chapter 3
The Lau Weight Shift System

Technically, the Lau Weight Shift System came to popularity after Ted Williams documented his Rotation Hitting System in *The Science of Hitting*, published in 1970. But for the sake of continuity, Lau should be studied as an extension of Early Weight Shift Theory.

Employing modern methods of photography, a modernizing of the weight shift system was undertaken by Charlie Lau in the 1970s. Lau made an extensive study of hitting, comparing old hitters with new, successful hitters with unsuccessful, home run hitters with high average hitters. He recognized many commonalities among the good hitters and, with the aid of an analytical mind, pieced together a superior weight shift system to cope with modern elements—lighter bats, the live ball, and stronger, faster hitters. His method essentially adapted the ancient weight shift system to modern times. That he was successful is reflected not only by the exceptional hitters who improved under his tutelage, but also in the raised batting averages of every team he coached.

Bringing the javelin thrower and shot putter back into view, characterizing the Weight Shift System and the Rotation System respectively, Lau successfully brought both body actions together to produce improved quickness with a degree of increased power. However, the Lau method of weight shift cannot be considered a power hitting system by any stretch of the imagination. The emphasis of his upgraded system still remains batting average, although the rotation of the hips *around* a *rigid front leg* offers the hitter more of an opportunity to pull the ball than the ancient weight shift system.

Lau retains the pronounced back-to-front weight shift, level swing, and front-arm dominance of the swing. His modifications are not so much focused on altering movement as on new concepts, many of which were either overlooked or not included in original weight shift theory.

Lau's emphasis is on several key points:

1. Balance, rhythm, and relaxation. Lau wants the hitter to accentuate a tension-free stance and swing execution for efficiency. With an absence of tension, balance and rhythm are allowed to assert themselves so the resulting swing is more of a natural, effortless movement. Tension and loss of balance are enemies to his system. The Lau Weight Shift System depends on *rhythm* of the forward weight shift for bat speed and power.

2. An aggressive, controlled stride which goes directly at the pitcher, causing the weight shift to be an attacking movement.

3. The front leg becomes "rigid" in accepting the weight transfer. This rigidity offers the shifting hip structure an opportunity to pivot *around* (not against) the front leg, much like a gate around a pole. This front leg *does not* offer resistance against the hip structure, but simply allows it to rotate if need be. Lau correctly insists that all hitters hit off their front leg rather than the rear leg (weight finishing over front leg rather than rear leg).

4. The hitter releases the top hand after contact and his head remains locked on the strike zone. This prevents the head from pulling off the ball by halting the shoulder rotation. Releasing the top hand after contact also stops trunk rotation and allows for a good jump out of the box. More, releasing the top hand allows full-extension of the front arm, regarded by Lau to be vital.

5. Preliminary movement. Lau wants the hitter to acquire inertia-busting movement prior to starting the swing. In his words, "You've got to go back in order to go forward." This involves a slight "backing" or "coiling" action to shift the weight backward before it starts forward into the weight shift.

6. Lau gives several reasons for not hitting the pitch out in front of the plate, and he preferred contact over the plate rather than in front of it on all but inside pitches. This allows use of the whole field.

7. Lau likes his hitter's front arm to finish "high." This is so the front arm has maximum forward extension in the follow-through. It also negates the "roll over" action of the top hand.

After it passes the point of contact, the top hand can release the bat while the front arm continues to pull it around in follow-through and the "high finish." If the top hand is *not* released, the front arm cannot extend fully. Also, if the rear arm (top hand) remains on the bat all the way through the follow-through it will continue to pull around the shoulders and trunk and eventually the head, which would be pulled off the ball. By releasing the top hand, the head can remain fixed on the point of contact.

Lau's high finish. Note angled shoulder rotation.

In constructing his hitting style, Lau essentially adds emphasis to many of the original weight shift characteristics, giving them new meaning, and adds the top hand release, high finish (for front arm extension), and the preliminary movement action.

Hallmarks of the Lau Weight Shift System: **1)** an aggressive weight shift; **2)** added hip rotation around a rigid front leg; **3)** a level swing; **4)** front arm extension.

Stance

Weight shift stances.

Deep crouch weight shift stance. Jackknifed body position can result in uneven shoulder rotation during the swing, which in turn can lead to chasing low pitches.

The Lau system emphasizes balance, although this hitter characteristically has more weight over his back leg than his front leg in more of a 60-40 to 90-10 weight distribution. Lau preferred both feet on a line pointing to the pitcher, neither "closed" nor "open".

Lau prefers a pronounced bend in the knees and waist, emphasizing balance from this position. The head tends to be over the toes of the rear foot in this position, or even further out if a deeper crouch is used. However, as the hitter crouches deeply he may tilt the body as he jack-knifes at the waist. If he does this he throws the alignment of his body in different directions and can cause the body to work against itself as it rotates unevenly.

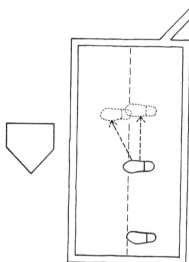

Feet are parallel to each other. Also, the stance is taken deep in the box, away from the plate. This is for better plate coverage when hitting the pitch over the middle and outside parts of the plate.

Lau's disciples tend to hold the bat higher in the stance, around shoulder level. This would seem proper, since this position affords the beginnings of a level swing—which Lau preferred—as the rotating shoulders can guide the bat more into a level plane. For hitters who prefer to hold the bat lower, in a position to uppercut, Lau had no argument. He deferred to the hitter's judgment in producing balance and naturalness. Lau specified a "flat" bat angle of no more than 45 degrees, however, and was agreeable to a bat angle approaching horizontal.

Mechanics of the Lau Weight Shift System

The unlocking sequence of body positions into a coordinated swing is the essence of the Lau Weight Shift System of hitting. Read carefully to follow the sequence.

To overcome rigidity, Lau emphasized that "a hitter must go back to go forward." This means that the hitter undergoes a rhythmic "rock" backward, shifting his weight further over the back leg until the batter's full weight rests here. This preliminary shift is done with a small knee-cock. This results in a "coiling" action which places the hitter's full weight against a rigid back leg and starts his rhythm.

The Lau knee cock.

Stride with closed front toe.

From this position the hitter thrusts his weight forward into the weight shift. Lau emphasizes that the stride is taken with the *front toe closed* as a key. This toe position keeps the hitter from opening his hips too early.

Again, Lau refers to the forward weight shift as "aggressive" and forceful. He realizes the stride is the power element of his system, and he wants it to be strong, attacking, although not wild or lunging. When the weight reaches the front leg, a *rigid* front leg, much like a pole, takes the weight and *holds* it. That is, the front leg does not aggressively repel the weight; it accepts the weight in an effort *to keep it where it is*. With the front leg accepting the weight shift, the hips can rotate adequately but considerably less forcibly than in Williams' Rotation System. The hips "glide" open rather than "snap" open.

Lau hip turn around rigid front leg.

With this aggressive weight shift comes momentum for the hands to swing the bat. Lau pounds home the point that when the front foot plants sideways, the hitter's hands are in the "launching position," or, positioned in their furthest place away from home plate. *The launching position is attained when the hitter strides away from his hands.* The hitter strides forward but the hands stay where they are.

Charlie Lau's description of the launching position: "In the launching position, the hands are back. The bottom hand is on a line drawn across the letters on the chest. This puts the top hand just off the tip of your rear shoulder. The bat is above the shoulder at about a 45 degree angle."

This launching position is the same for any hitting style, with the hands locked in their strongest starting position.

The front arm provides direction for a level swing, aided by the rotating action of the torso and front shoulder. Lau does not indicate which arm provides the most force. He says both work together to get the bat to the contact zone. After contact the top hand releases and the front arm continues to pull the bat into an elongated arc with extension of the front arm. Lau prefers the hitter to finish "high" with the front arm. This is to insure front arm extension. The head remains locked on the contact zone. This, combined with the "closed toe" landing position of the striding foot, causes hip action to be slightly restricted, opening close to 90 degrees but usually falling just short of full hip turn.

Walt Hriniak, leading Lau theorist, on keeping the head down during the swing and follow through: "The head stays down, looking at the ball as it passes below the head, to see it as long as possible. Like Boggs. If you watch him closely you'll see his head stay down on the contact area a long, long time, even after the ball has left the bat. And Hank Aaron did the same thing."

The Launching Position. High hands allow the bat to go down through the strike zone.

Head remains down on contact zone after contact.

33

When executed properly, the weight shift hitter feels a connection of energy from the weight shift into the arms as the bat comes through. This is a coordination of energy from all body parts, much like a well executed golf swing. Balance is maintained by the rigid front leg collecting the weight, although a slight forward tilt of the body may continue beyond the balance point, which is a result of the weight shift inertia.

In total, the entire movement is tension-free and rhythmic. Power comes from the lower half of the body via the weight shift being held and opened by the rigid front leg. The front arm directs the swing to the contact area.

A point of contention, as far as bat speed is concerned, centers on the arm action. Lau never specifies the dominant arm of his system, although he unwittingly gives an edge to the front arm by allowing it to extend in the high finish, while cutting short the top arm's extension by releasing it after contact. Thus, the thrust of extension is given to the front arm rather than the rear arm. Like the Early Weight Shift System, this mechanism will leave the barrel of the bat in the path of the ball longer, increasing contact, but reduce the advantage of rear arm strength.

Walt Hriniak: "I think the most important hand in hitting is the bottom hand. I don't believe in the top hand theory. If the top hand works too much it will roll the bat out of the way of the ball. We emphasize the bottom hand so the top hand doesn't have to do too much of the work."

Another Lau tenet requires discussion as it pertains to the purpose of Lau's system. In his book, *The Art of Hitting .300*, he states, "Gear yourself to the ball away and let the inside pitch take care of itself." Given that the inside pitch is the rotation hitter's "power pitch," this would suggest that Lau preferred plate coverage and average to power, as is also suggested by the title of his book. "Gear yourself to the ball away" means that the forward weight shift "slide," and front arm dominance, are geared for this outside pitch. If the pitch is inside, a split-second, on-the-spot adjustment can then be attempted by 1) pushing against the rigid front leg and using a bit more of the available hip rotation, and 2) switching to rear arm dominance from front arm dominance.

This adjustment from outside plate coverage to inside plate coverage is covered more thoroughly in Chapter 6, "Stroke Adaptions: Adapting From Outside Plate Coverage to Inside Pitches."

Head Movement

Forward movement caused by the weight shift can be measured in these photos by the player's head in relation to the pole behind him. A) Hitter begins in classical weight shift stance with the majority of weight over the back leg. B) Front foot lands with toe closed, swing begins. C) Weight shift continues as the bat comes forward. D) Hitter finishes with weight continuing over front leg. Total head movement is equal to the distance between the feet.

Another feature of the Lau Weight Shift System requires discussion. That is head movement. In the Lau Weight Shift System, the head travels nearly as far as that of the Early Weight Shift hitter. An aggressive weight shift over a rigid, accepting front leg is a long way for the head to travel in the direction of the pitch. The distance covered by an aggressive weight shift can be as much as two or three feet, from start to finish. The velocity which the head and eyes travel forward must be added to the velocity of the pitch to calculate the velocity which the hitter's eyes are seeing.

Richie Zisk: "You're making the pitcher faster than he really is when the head travels forward a lot. And any time the body moves, the eyes move. When the eyes move, the ball takes a bad hop on the way in."

Advantages of the Lau System

1. High batting average, fewer strikeouts, more contact.

2. All field contact, although pulling the inside pitch requires exceptional adjusting movement and coordination.

3. Good jump out of the batter's box due to forward momentum of weight shift and restricted hip rotation. The weight shift can be converted into the first stride toward first base by simply bending the knee and continuing the forward momentum.

4. Increased bat speed for the hitter without much strength in his hands and arms comes from the thrust from lower body weight shift.

5. Crouched batting position puts the eyes closer to the pitch.

6. Because of emphasis on weight shift over hand speed, this hitter is most effective on the pitch from the middle of the plate out.

7. With the front leg rigid holding the weight shift, the hips have a chance to turn adequately to handle the inside pitch if reactions are quick enough.

Disadvantages of the Lau System

1. Hand speed is sacrificed by the top arm leaving the bat in a less than fully extended position, in favor of front arm extension. Loss of some arm and hand strength and power.

2. For the hitter with hand and arm strength, emphasis on lower body shift and front arm extension reduces his power assets. Power is sacrificed for contact.

Question to **Al Kaline:** Do you think the weight shift method is good for the power hitter?

Kaline: "No, I don't. I think it really hurts a lot of guys who could hit for power. It helps some become better hitters for average, but one of the reasons is that the pitchers aren't afraid to pitch to them because the best they'll do is hit a single.

"Lead arm [weight shift] hitters are not as effective in the upper part of the strike zone. To hit the high pitch effectively, the top hand needs to take an active role."

3. Weakness on the high strike, inside pitches, and hard throwers.

4. If the hitter releases the top hand during the swing, the front arm can be coaxed into extending another six or eight inches into bad-ball hitting territory. Worse, should the hitter change his mind and try to hold up his swing, releasing the top hand means loss of a "safety chord" in holding the bat back.

5. Exaggerated forward head movement. The speed of the forward stride must be added to the pitch velocity to calculate what the eyes see.

6. Because of the emphasis on lower body movement, slightly restricted hip rotation, and front arm extension, the system is more conducive to left-handerd hitting than right-handed hitting (covered more thoroughly in Chapter 6).

7. Because of the upward pulling action of the front arm going into a high finish, weight shift hitters have a tendency to hit top-spin line drives which can have a dampening effect on "contact velocity". Also, top spin ground balls have a tough time getting through the infield. Only if the hitter can manage to level out his swing will he get the maximum contact velocity produced with backspin.

Right-handed hitters have used this system to improve, but the overwhelming majority of successful weight shift hitters, including those using the Lau Method, have been left-handed hitters.

The Lau method, in its entirety, can be hard on power hitters, particularly right-handed ones, who cannot use their full hip rotation to get their power. And, almost universally, hip rotation requires (or commands) rear arm, not front arm, extension (review page 15 photos of top and bottom hand use.) A safe hitting statement could be that hip rotation and rear arm extension are dependent upon and linked to each other, while front arm extension is indispensable to weight shift. Crossing these features would not result in what Lau would call rhythmic, balanced, natural. The hitter must decide which pair he wants.

Since Charlie Lau passed away in 1985, the system has continued to be taught by his disciples, the most notable being Walt Hriniak of the Chicago White Sox. As such, Hriniak shoulders the responsibility for teaching the system to coaches and players, as well as answering the critics.

Walt Hriniak: "One thing Charlie and I have always been accused of is that we teach everybody to hit the same way. That's not true at all. Sure there's a shift in weight, sure you've got to go back to go forward, sure there's a good follow-through, and there are certain ways to make these happen. It's all an individual thing and our system allows for individual differences in each hitter.

"If done properly, the weight shift doesn't come until the swing happens. When the stride is taken, the weight hasn't shifted forward yet. It's more of a 50-50 movement. We start back, we make our move to the ball with the legs, our stride is completed. At this point, the weight is distributed equally. Then the weight shift occurs as the swing is completed.

Sam Rice with early top hand release.

"Once the ball is hit we feel the job isn't done. There has to be a good follow-through. We emphasize a good strong finish either by releasing the top hand from the bat or keeping both hands on the bat and finishing above the shoulder. If the top hand is released, well that's something which has been done for a hundred years, Speaker to Strawberry."

Hriniak: "All hitters use a weight shift. Some more forward, some less, but they all move forward. Stop Williams or Reggie Jackson at contact and they have moved forward significantly. We're about at the same point at contact. After the ball leaves the bat, they [rotation hitters] recoil against the front leg and lean back. We continue forward and break into our stride."

Lau's version of weight shift is a much improved version of hitting, and for the hitter with only average strength, particularly if he has foot speed and is left-handed, this system is ideal. Incorporations of Lau's hitting tenets have adapted the Weight Shift System to be successful in modern times to the point where many consider it the best hitting system in use. Still, one must ask, would Gehrig or DiMaggio have been the same hitters using a pure weight shift system?

Chapter 4
The Williams Rotation System

H allmarks: **1)** limited weight shift; **2)** full hip rotation; **3)** rear arm dominance; **4)** an uppercut stroke.

Envision the shot putter. He characterizes the Rotation Hitting System not just by using his legs and torso to generate power via rotation, but also by close rear arm positioning and upward, extending action of the rear arm.

The Rotation System was documented in 1970 with Ted Williams' book, *The Science of Hitting*. Williams is its sole spokesman with no predecessors, although hitters and hitting instructors had both been using this knowledge and passing it along for decades. Nonetheless, until Williams' concise documentation the Rotation System, in its entirety, did not exist. Many people regard it as an older hitting system because of the Lau resurgence of weight shift in the seventies, but the Rotation System is the newer of the two hitting systems. It evolved with the advent of the live ball and lighter bats which could be "whipped" rather than "dragged." Hitters were realizing that with the combination of live ball, lighter bat, and a slight uppercut, baseballs could be hit consistently for distance. New, streamlined mechanics were required to get the job done. Some strong hitters, two of the first being Babe Ruth and Hack Wilson, felt the whole process of hitting could become energy efficient when the ball was pulled to the power field. No longer were three hits required to score a single run. Instead of hitting and running out of the box, now they could hit it and trot, and get paid more money in the process.

Hack Wilson.

It is safe to say that no home run hitter ever used a pure weight shift system because of the restrictions to power. The Rotation System is the home run hitting system. Singles, center field contact, and high average are not the goal of the Rotation System hitter. This system employs a stance and mechanical movement suited for power and bat speed.

The reader should note that each body position and movement of the Rotation System hitter is diametrically opposed in both meaning and result to the Weight Shift System. The bottom line is this: to any body position or action which retards the swing of the weight shift hitter, the rotation hitter employs an opposite position or action to increase the speed of the swing. That in mind, I often refer to the Rotation System action as a stroke, rather than a swing.

Stance

Like the Lau method, the Rotation method can be used from any stance. However, we go to Williams for a description of the classical rotation stance. Rear foot is parallel to the end line of the batters box, but the front foot is opened slightly, 20 or 30 degrees, toward the pitcher. This is to facilitate hip rotation when the time comes. Feet are on a line pointing to the pitcher, or slightly open. The position in the box is closer to home plate than weight shift hitters, so the hitter will have more inside strikes which he can "rotate into."

Initially, the weight of the hitter is evenly distributed, with neither leg supporting more weight than the other.

Body position is upright, vertical, or what is called a "stacked" body position—body segments stacked on top of each other like a totem pole or a stack of pancakes. This is because rotating a vertical axis is physically more efficient than rotating one which is jackknifed in different directions.

Hands and bat are held below shoulder level and close to the rib cage, nearly in contact with the body. This position allows full use of the Law of Conservation of Angular Momentum—close limbs facilitate rapid axis rotation. The bat angle is vertical, as much for Williams' preference as its only possible angle with the hands low and close to the body.

Note vertical stance and bat position, low hands and open front foot.

Mechanical Action

From the Rotation System stance, as laid down by Williams, two movements occur for the purpose of gaining *kinetic* energy. Williams employs these movements to *prepare* the way for hip rotation and bat speed. These movements, equivalent to Lau's "preliminary movement," need considerable practice and repetition for mastery.

The first of the initial movements is Williams' knee cock. From its position in the stance, the front knee turns inward four to ten inches or so. Like Lau's preliminary movement, this accomplishes two things. *One*, the knee-turn puts the hip structure in a coiled, cocked position, braced against the back leg, loading it with kinetic power. *Two*, the knee-turn effectively transfers the body's weight to the back leg. This essentially puts the hitter in a favorable weight shift position, except that he has *gained the kinetic potential of cocked hips*. With this action, Williams is mimicking the pitcher's action.

What does the pitcher do? He lifts his striding leg, cocks his hips, weight goes to the back leg, then he thrusts this position forward onto a firm front leg. Williams does this in miniature.

Some hitters, like Kirby Puckett, Cal Ripken, and Reuben Sierra cock their hips with nearly as much leg turn as the pitcher. Use of this much body action will increase rotational power but much practice is needed to work it with timing and control.

Simultaneously with the knee-turn, Williams employed a hitch, a hand "pump," or a slight "twitch" of the bat, to give the bat movement and overcome its state of inertia. This may tilt the barrel of the bat toward the plate and back to initiate movement. With this, the bat is given momentum, *lightening* it, so that when the stroke begins, it comes through the hitting zone faster.

Cecil Fielder dropping his hands in hitching movement timed to his knee cock. If the hitter uses downward hitching hand action he should return his hands to the high starting position before the bat comes forward.

43

As a result of the leg turn, the weight is now *against* the back leg, hips cocked, bat in motion. Now the stride begins. As in the weight shift, the back leg pushes the weight forward into a weight shift, using a stride of only six inches to a foot. The front foot lands pointing in approximately the same thirty to 45 degree angle in which it started in the stance. The instant the striding foot plants, weight shift is *finished,* and *rotation begins.*

Rotation System Hip Action

Rear leg pushes hips open 45 degrees. Front leg pushes hips into 90 degree rotation.

As the hips pivot to face the pitcher, the front foot also pivots to face the pitcher. Both legs supply equal power for hip rotation. It happens like this: the back leg has pushed the rear side of the hip structure into weight shift, opening up the hips 45 degrees. Now the front foot plants and pushes the front side of the hip structure *backward* into 90 degrees of rotation.

When both legs are planted, pushing on opposite sides of the hips, the hands begin working. The back arm is positioned in the stance like the fist of a boxer, pushing forward out of the trunk rotation toward the pitcher. This is a sideways *pressing* forward action by the rear arm, and a tight extending action by the front arm. Both arms flow out of the body rotation, from the body axis toward the strike zone. Not in an arc of front-to-back, but more in a line from body-to-strike-zone.

Both arms, but particularly the back arm because of its anatomical advantage, are extended by the triceps with the help of the shoulder muscles. The rear arm gives a powerful push forward into full extension and finishes its work with a roll-over follow-though. Both hands remain on the bat throughout the majority of the stroke (Ripken).

Cal Ripken.

Wade Boggs.

Because the top hand stays on the bat, the front arm cannot fully extend. In the Rotation System the rear arm extension gets priority over front arm extension, opposite Weight Shift System arm action (Boggs).

Balance is maintained by gyroscopic stability—equal force leaving the rotation on all sides simultaneously. What balance is lost in this system will be due to minute shifts of weight depending on the location of the pitch, which are controlled by the balls of the feet.

The Uppercut

Uppercut Dynamics.

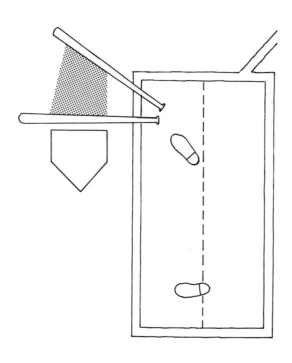

As the trunk rotates and the shoulders open to face the pitcher, the low slung hands have no choice but to be pulled upward by the higher shoulder attachment. This guarantees an uppercut.

Additionally, when the vertical position of the bat barrel is lowered into an arc, *gravity* pulls the barrel below the hands temporarily before the hands regain control and force the bat back into the arc. This makes for a warped path into the strike zone, further accenting the uppercut.

The point of contact for the Rotation System hitter is in front of the plate, where it can be pulled with power.

Advantages of the Rotation System

1. Increased bat speed and power afforded by full hip rotation, top hand extension, and close held arms. Contact is explosive because of the tight arc and bat speed.

2. By leaving the rear arm on the bat throughout the arm extension, the front arm cannot extend the bat into bad ball hitting territory. Also, the top hand affords the "safety cord" aspect to help pull the bat back on a checked swing.

3. The head does not move forward drastically. Once the front foot plants, weight shift stops and so does forward head movement. The head does not rush into the pitch velocity.

No rotation head movement. Measure from home plate.

4. The rotation hitter, with his bat speed, is effective on pitches from the middle of the plate inward. With the increased rotation and bat speed, he can usually drive these pitches.

5. The Rotation System is more conducive to right-handed hitting than the Weight Shift System because of its capacity for more quickness. Also, the left-handed hitter is not penalized in any way in this system. (See Chapter 6, "Left-handed Versus Right-handed Hitting.")

Disadvantages of the Rotation System

Less square, center field contact. Strikeouts are increased. This is because the tight, high-speed, quick-ending arc produced by the Rotation System is in and out of the strike zone for a shorter length of time.

2. Less contact means more strikeouts, lower average, and less center field contact—the least populated area of the field.

3. Difficulty with the outside pitch. Again, the pitch over the outside half is farther away, and with more distance comes more time. Thus, to hit this pitch effectively the Rotation System hitter must slow his bat down (immeasurably) to center this pitch, a difficult thing to do. Also, it is next to impossible to center the outside pitch consistently with an uppercut.

4. Because he rotates against the front leg and ends up with his rotating momentum going away from the field, the hitter gets a poor jump out of the batter's box.

5. The small, fast man employing Rotation System characteristics works against himself by trying to hit the long ball rather than going for line drives, center field contact, and leg hits.

Last, it is wise to understand that only players physically blessed with strength can take

Dave Justice in weight shift follow-through.   *Sam Horn in rotation follow-through.*

full advantage of pure rotation style hitting. Nonetheless, the smart hitter can use several of its features to quicken his bat and shore up difficulties and temporary problems if he understands the principles of this dynamic system.

Chapter 5
A Third Force:
The Combined System

"We all have some rotation and weight shift in us. Anybody that takes a stride and turns their hips is doing both. I'm a weight shift guy and a rotation guy. I think it's a combination."
—*Ben Hines, Los Angeles Dodgers*

Lau   Schmidt   Williams

Does it not stand to reason that if we have two complete and successful hitting systems adapted to modern times, each with advantages and disadvantages, the advantages could be combined, the drawbacks discarded, and a system superior to both would be in the works? Couldn't we synergize the best features and steer clear of features which do not suit a given hitter? These are thoughts worth examining.

It should come as no surprise that every hitter combines elements from both systems. Hank Aaron was a great example. Aaron was a master at both hitting systems, and could shift in and out of a particular system in mid-stroke. This can be seen in many of his action photos, particularly in his follow-through. Depending on when the photographer snaps him, he may be in a weight shift follow-through or a rotation follow-through. Will Clark is another one. I used to watch him from my third base view.

Hank Aaron.

He has a "model" weight shift stance, preliminary actions, and weight transfer. He hits the ball over the center of the plate to all fields. His leg will take the weight and push off to first base. But if the pitch is inside, his front leg stops the weight shift and he converts to rotation. His style includes the best of both systems.

As my career went along, I found myself doing the same things as Aaron, depending on the location of the pitch. This is not something I told myself to do, it was the result of action. I'm saying that this combination movement evolved into a style all its own from all the physical and mental data I accumulated over my entire career. I didn't do the combining, it just happened. It happened because, in their pure forms, I found that neither the Weight Shift System nor the Rotation System could be universally applied.

Let me describe the factors which evolved my hitting into something between Lau and Williams. First, a Combined Hitting System is the result of not being locked into a particular hitting system. I started out a rotation hitter, then became a weight shift hitter, and finally settled between them. Second, it is based on the majority percentages of the most likely hitting variables. Third, it addresses the three key elements in hitting —contact, bat speed, and power; and fourth, how the hitter can get optimum hitting production by combining average and power.

Majority Percentages

In constructing this Combined System, we begin with the *majority percentages* of what is most likely to happen to a hitter. In other words, no hitter can prepare himself for every possibility, every trick a pitcher can use. If he could, balance would be gone from the game. What the hitter must do is prepare his thinking and actions to the most likely, the percentage choice, the *middle ground.* "Avoid the extremes," is how **Charlie Lau** put it. I say he's right.

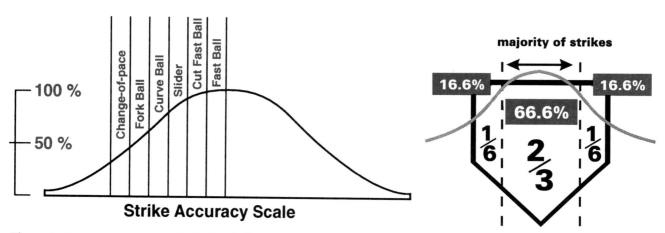

The majority percentages are with the fast ball crossing the middle two-thirds of the plate.

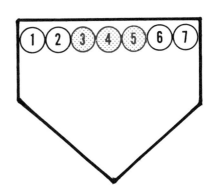

Zisk's area of concentration.

Richie Zisk has a great visual concept of "avoiding the extremes." **Zisk:** "I personally feel that the hitter should look for the ball *in the center of the strike zone* and make adjustments off of that. Seven baseballs will cover the plate, black to black. And if we gear our swing for the two balls on the inner part of the plate, we become vulnerable to the five balls on the other side, and vice versa. That's a five ball adjustment for a two ball advantage. But if we're looking for the three balls in the middle, the adjustments in or out are much less drastic.

"Hitting is adjustment, so to begin you want to handle where the ball will be a majority of the time."

I feel the same way. I geared myself for the ball in the majority portion of the plate—over the middle. And with two strikes, I looked from the fourth to the seventh ball.

The Essential Hitting Elements

In further defining the Combined Hitting System, we must isolate the essential hitting elements and consult the physical and anatomical principles as they apply. The essential hitting elements, those which qualify the hitter as effective, are *contact, bat speed,* and *power.* Optimum methods to achieve these must be our focus.

Contact

In the vast majority of cases, the pitcher's most reliable weapon, his "percentage" pitch, is his fast ball. So the hitter gears the plane of his swing, and his thinking, to this pitch. Fast balls sink, rise, fade, or tail, but these movements tend to be minimal in comparison to breaking balls. Fast balls are the straightest pitch your opponent will throw. Because the fast ball movement will be the closest to straight, and somewhat unpredictable, we can initially consider it as *straight.*

Ted Williams has made a case for the pitcher's fast ball following a downward path from the pitcher's hand, to justify his uppercut. I'm going to take exception to Ted's case.

True, the pitch is released from a ten-inch mound from a six-foot man, which dictates a higher point of release than the strike zone. But the vast *majority* of pitchers throw from a three-quarters release, putting their release point at about cap height. Also, the pitcher's stride puts him lower on the mound by almost half his height.

The pitcher's leg drive drops his height and release point considerably.

More, the pitcher's stride puts him lower on the mound by half the height of the mound, five inches. If he releases the ball from around head high now, the release point is actually closer to *only five feet higher* than home plate. With the heart of the strike zone around three feet high, the downward angle of the pitch is modified considerably. Further, the center field camera shows unmistakably that the *majority* of pitcher's fast balls thrown from the three-quarters release tend to *level off* as they arrive at home plate, due to the spin imparted by the three-quarters release. This leveling off action of the fast ball nullifies the higher release point in a *majority* of cases.

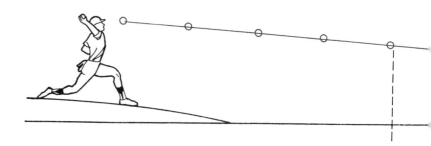

The majority of fast balls tend to level off on the way to home plate.

To make contact with the pitcher's truest weapon, the fast ball, the majority of which level off in flight, a *level swing* aimed in the direction of that flight would produce maximum contact. No hitter's entire swing is perfectly level but, using proper top hand action, *the middle of the swing can be*, and the closer he comes the more contact he will produce and the more productive he will be.

The level swing is valuable because the barrel of the bat is on a direct collision course with the ball, and allows the hitter to be a bit late or early and still make square, line drive contact. How can this be achieved?

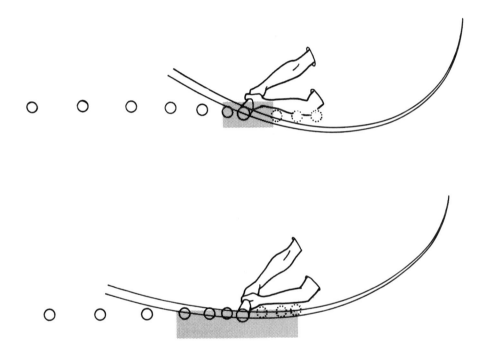

Level swing fast ball contact area versus uppercut fast ball contact area.

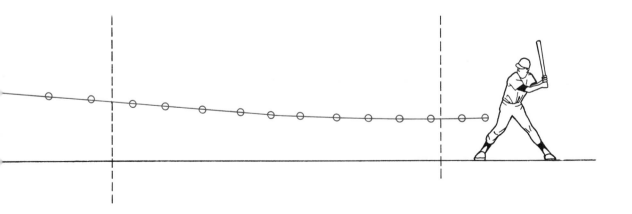

Charlie Lau: "To produce a level swing, you have to get on top of the ball [hands begin the swing above the ball's flight] by swinging down at it. Even with the proper weight shift, many hitters still have a tendency toward a slight uppercut, which, as long as it remains slight, isn't all that bad. The problems occur when the uppercut is an extreme loop. That's what you want to avoid, and getting on top of the ball and swinging down is a good way to counteract this tendency. Ideally, the two motions will cancel each other out and the result is a level swing."

Cal Ripken starts high to come down through the strike zone. Note level plane of bat and top hand action.

THE COMBINED SYSTEM:
A) Level Cut

I couldn't agree more. Visualize the swing plane. The closer this plane comes to a perfectly horizontal straight line, the better hitter you will be. And for the hitter, *level means down.* The more level the swing plane, the larger area of square contact.

Every hitter has a natural uppercut because the arms attach at the shoulder and the bat comes through thigh high or so. Sure a perfectly level plane is impossible, from start to finish. But in the middle of the swing plane, through the contact area, *the bat can travel perfectly level,* before the arms take it back up to shoulder length.

There's another reason for uppercutting. Habit. Every boy developed a natural uppercut from the first days he ever hit a wiffle ball as a youngster. The pitch came in from a high arc to low so he swung up to meet it. And to a youngster, fly balls are exciting. To a pro player concerned with his production, they're depressing. *Now* is the time to change! Take it from Lau and me.

We know that Williams initiates his uppercut via two means: 1) low hands which are pulled up by the rotating shoulders, and; 2) a vertical bat angle upon which gravity acts to warp the swing. So we must stay away from these if we want the bat to travel on a level path to the *percentage* straight pitch.

Borrowing from the Weight Shift System, Lau in particular, we know that a higher placement of the hands will be pulled across by the rotating shoulder in a more level manner. And gravity cannot affect a flatter bat angle nearly as much. These two positions allow the bat to go *down and across* the strike zone easier, as opposed to *up into* it by low slung hands. This means that while both *ends* of the swing may not be level, the *center* of the swing, in the contact area, *can be perfectly level* if you use proper top hand action.

Hand and wrist action of the level cut

The weight shift theorists have a strong argument for guiding the barrel of the bat through the strike zone on an *elongated arc* for maximum contact, and more square, center field contact. This action is mindful of the tennis player pushing the face of his racket at a rocket serve (and getting square contact), or the golfer pushing the face of his putter at the golf ball for *accuracy*. By *pressing* the hands forward ahead of the barrel of the bat, the hitter can change the direction of his swing ever so slightly into an elongated arc on a collision course with the pitch. **Ted Williams** describes the swing this way on page 58 of his classic, *The Science of Hitting*: "The baseball swing is a hard push-swing. The wrists roll after the ball has left the bat."

This pushing, or pressing, element is most easily accomplished by hands fixed three to five inches or so off the rear shoulder, closer to the body's axis. This gives the hitter the feeling of violently pressing the bat into the strike zone *from the side*, rather than pulling it through from back to front.

Rear arm (top hand) push action into the ball. The bat is "pushed" into the contact position. Extension takes place well after the ball is hit. This swing resulted in a home run.

Ben Hines describes the action as "keeping the hands inside the flight of the pitch" during the swing, or, going from inside the flight of the ball to the strike zone. This is the essence of the pressing or "shoving" action. Confirming **Hines'** advice, Darren Daulton told me recently that he owes his new found success to learning to swing "inside the flight of the pitch." This is an "inside out" action—from *inside* the flight of the pitch *to* the flight of the pitch. It accomplishes four important things: 1) this shortens the stroke so the hitter can both wait longer and be quicker; 2) it guarantees maximum use of the hands; 3) it "squares" the bat for maximum collision with the pitch and; 4) this "squared" contact negates the hazards of pulling and directs hit balls toward center field, which is the least populated area of the diamond.

Don't let my description confuse you. The "pushing" action described here is not the pure inside-out swing you might think it is. If you will place your hands in the stance position and simulate your swing in slow motion you will see the top arm actually passes in front of the chest *pushing* as the bottom hand is pulling. The top arm is in a bent "L" position. This movement will produce singles or home runs depending on strength and size of the hitter and his bat speed. The bat speed is a result of the push of the rear arm and the pull of the front arm. And since you can push harder than you can pull, the top arm gives the strongest force. Rather than a pure "push," it becomes a "push-swing."

Ben Hines' concept of keeping the hands inside the flight of the pitch.

THE COMBINED SYSTEM:
A) **Level Cut**
B) **Center Field Contact**

Bat Speed

Many people compare the golf swing to the baseball swing under the guise that what is good for one must be good for the other. They like to emphasize the front side initiating the swing. And without exception they overlook one vital difference, *time*. Don't forget, the pitcher is programmed to ruin timing with an assortment of tricks. The hitter cannot always be smooth, precise, gliding, waiting for everything to come together like the golfer can. The hitter's mechanics will always be in varying mechanical sequence when suddenly, he has to *strike*. Therefore, his *hands* must make up for timing glitches. The better the hand action, the more timing mistakes can be overcome. And . . .

The faster a hitter can swing the bat, the longer he can wait to judge the pitch.

We know that the hitter must swing the bat with at least the same velocity as the pitch or imprecise contact will be feeble. To get bat speed, the top hand imparts a strong "snap" forward after it "push-swings" through the contact zone. This strongly suggests that top hand action must get into the swing.

Al Kaline: "I used to guide pretty much with my bottom hand and use my top hand when I wanted to generate power and quickness to the ball."

Power

The inclusion of power in any hitting style ushers in several questions. Will power upset timing and rhythm? Will it reduce the chances of square contact? Is it necessary to the hitter interested in batting average? Power elements should not be included for the sole purpose of hitting home runs, unless that is the strong hitter's goal. Yet from the standpoint of doing the most with a given pitch, gaining bat speed, and delivering blows into the gaps, denying power elements would be self-defeating. Therefore, on the basis of delivering more bat speed and time to the hitter, and helping team production with long hits, some power elements can be included for the combination hitter. There is one exception to the power, however. Taking into consideration the level cut, the push-swing element, and looking over the center to outside half of the plate, this power should be directed straight away, from left-center field to right-center field. Should the power result elsewhere the hitter will gladly take it, but striving to pull the ball would defeat his purpose of combining average and power.

A perfect example is Darren Daulton. He tried to power pull his entire career. In 1992 his home runs began going to left and left center, less to

THE COMBINED SYSTEM:
    A) **Level Cut**
    B) **Center Field Contact**
    C) **Top Hand Force**

his pull field. He had a year like never before, 27 home runs, 109 RBI, and he hit .270. In my opinion, all this happened because he directed his power to center field by swinging inside the flight of the pitch and "squaring" his contact. Darren saw a new hitting concept. It took him a long time, and it did for me, too. A lot of learning comes by watching successful men and following their lead, and this is probably what Darren did. My models were Dick Allen, Hank Aaron, and Roberto Clemente. Their teaching was simple. What they did, I did.

Harry Walker, hitting coach *par excellence*, has made a fine video on batting. At the end of his video he has included some priceless, rare, slow motion footage of the great ones—Ruth, Musial, Gehrig, Kiner, Waner. What I see in this footage, to the man, are great examples of *weight shift plus rotation*, much like the Lau weight shift only with a bit more rotation. Let's ask ourselves, can we duplicate the actions of these great hitters?

Don Mattingly rotating against angled front leg.

If the hitter gathers his weight against his back leg and takes a comfortable, healthy stride, he has produced the weight shift. Now, if he can provide resistance to the weight shift by firming up his front leg, he will rotate the weight shift, as Lau proves. Now, if he will maintain his front leg *on a slight backward angle*, perhaps only 10 to 15 degrees, he will get more rotating action without pushing the hip structure backward into full rotation. This simply adds a slight backward angle to Lau's weight shift. Two simple actions will do it—the forward flow of the weight shift stopped by a rigid leg *angled backwards* ever so slightly. If you can maintain a level plane with your swing and this body action, you'll be an exceptionally good hitter.

Remember, the combination hitter will accomplish the most if he also gears his mechanics to the middle of the plate. He can then be effective on the majority of pitches which cross the plate. If the pitch is inside, he can make the instinctive adjustment to rotate the hips around the slightly angled rigid front leg. This way the hitter can switch from a weight shift hitter to a rotation hitter, depending on pitch location.

To get more power, the bottom half of the body comes into play. The hips can be cocked with a slight, Williams-style knee turn in a slow, preliminary shift of weight to the back leg. Add a slight hitch or twitch of the bat to overcome the bat's inertia and the hitter has coiled himself with kinetic power. (More on this coiling action in Lesson 3, Pre-swing Movement.)

Richie Zisk: "The loading of the hips, the coiling action, is very important. A lot of power is generated by the lower body. That power, coupled with hand action, is what results in the long ball. Ted Williams, Hank Aaron—great hip coil. Our guys, Sandberg, Andre Dawson, good hip coil and action."

Hitter Production

Take it from me, a reformed fly ball hitting expert, balls hit into the air are useless to personal and team production 90% of the time. The only exceptions are the rare fly ball home runs (not back-spin line drives), the equally rare fly ball that drops between fielders, and sacrifice flies. On the other hand, ground balls are useless only about 60% of the time. Only the ground ball that is fielded cleanly and doesn't move a runner up is useless. That's a 30% difference in production. Ask any manager and he'll tell you. He'll take the ground ball over the fly ball any day, any game, any inning. I'll say it this way: It is skillful hitting to be a ground ball/line drive hitter. That's what Al Oliver, Clemente, and Pete Rose were, and what I finally got to be. When I played against these guys, they were the toughest outs in the book. Man on third, less than two out, and they're up? Count the run.

Here are facts about the skill of hitting ground balls and low line drives: 1) it is only acquired with a level cut, and again, to the hitter level means down; 2) since the ideal contact swing angle is level, which occurs not at the beginning or the end of the swing, but in the middle, *contact should be made in the middle of the swing.* Where does that happen? Brace yourselves. It happens over home plate, not in front of it. Not to leave this statement hanging, this concept will be discussed in detail in Lesson 2: Hand Action. For now, we need only to know that ground balls and line drives directed toward center field are the most productive ways to hit.

Summary

The combination hitter is most effective on the middle two thirds of the plate. He strives to make contact over the front half of the plate, or, on the inside pitch, a couple of inches in front of it. He can adjust to the

THE COMBINED SYSTEM:
A) Level Cut
B) Center Field Contact
C) Top Hand Force
D) Angled Front Leg

THE COMBINED SYSTEM:
A) Level Cut
B) Center Field Contact
C) Top Hand Force
D) Angled Front Leg
E) Ground Ball/Line Drive Emphasis
F) Contact Made in the Middle (Level Portion) of the Swing

inside or outside pitches by controlling his weight shift with the angled front leg. Perhaps the finest example of a player blending the weight shift plus rotation for both power and average was George Foster, who in 1977 hit .320 with 52 home runs from the right side. He combined a long stride, full weight shift, angled front leg, and hit as many home runs to right and center as he did to left field.

Advantages of the Combined System

1. High average hitting is still attained. The level stroke allows for sufficient contact in the left center to right center field direction.

2. The top hand remains on the bat throughout extension for maximum force and the "safety chord" stays on to help check the swing.

3. The stroke is most effective for the middle two thirds of the plate—where the majority of pitches will be thrown.

4. Bat speed is still rapid with the rear arm adding force.

5. Power and adaptability is afforded by the hips opening the weight shift against an angled leg.

6. With the strength of the rear arm, the combination characteristics are conducive to both right-handed and left-handed hitters.

7. Head movement is minimized.

Disadvantages of the Combined System

1. Maximum power and bat speed are compromised slightly in favor of average and power combination.

2. The hitter is vulnerable to the inside and outside corners of the plate.

Cecil Fielder begins in a vertical rotation stance, falls back into a weight shift stance, then cocks his body with a knee turn and a hand pump.

Nearly every hitter today employs a combination of both the Weight Shift and Rotation Systems. George Brett at times hybridizes with accentuated hip rotation to pull the ball. Cecil Fielder, a home run specialist, employs a weight shift stance and directs his power to all fields. Will Clark goes back and forth depending on pitch location. They use elements from both hitting systems to accomplish their individual purposes. In Part 2 I will give you all the individual skills used in the Combined Hitting System.

Above all, do not regard the hitting actions as complicated and mystical. Often words are cumbersome in their descriptions, but the movements themselves are not. Ryne Sandberg is a good example.

Richie Zisk: "Ryne [Sandberg] keeps everything in its simplest terms. You watch him in batting practice and there is nothing complicated about it. The ball is thrown, his hips cock, the hands go back, the hips unwind, the hands come through, the head stays on the ball and whack. I mean, it's frighteningly simple. As uncomplicated as you can get."

Like Richie, I've always admired the simplicity of Ryne Sandberg's batting style. He has one of the most consistent level/down swing planes of any hitter I have ever seen. When he keeps the ball out of the air he's one of the toughest right-handed hitters in the game. A young hitter would not go wrong trying to imitate Ryne. His style hasn't changed since he was a minor leaguer with the Phillies. He keeps things basic and he's become a great hitter.

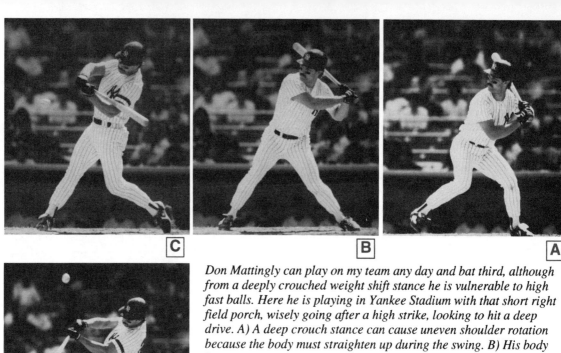

C

B

A

D

Don Mattingly can play on my team any day and bat third, although from a deeply crouched weight shift stance he is vulnerable to high fast balls. Here he is playing in Yankee Stadium with that short right field porch, wisely going after a high strike, looking to hit a deep drive. A) A deep crouch stance can cause uneven shoulder rotation because the body must straighten up during the swing. B) His body begins straightening up, led by the front shoulder. His launching position begins with high hands. C) Because the front shoulder lifts the body, uneven shoulder rotation results. The uneven shoulder rotation cancels out the top hand force. Cancelling top hand action makes him late to the strike zone. D) With top hand action cancelled, the bat head dips well below forearm level (see page 88). Don is late on a home run pitch. In this sequence Don has raised up nearly a foot with uneven shoulder rotation.

A

B

Here I'm also going for a high strike. A) Starting from the launch position my hands are high and back, gripping extremely firm and tightening the arm linkage. B) Bat approaching from high to level. C) Bat completes the level portion of the swing, eyes are locked on contact. Firm, angled front leg both accepts and resists weight shift. D) Top hand rolls over, neither arm gains complete extension, shoulders are rotating level. E) Finish is even with the shoulders.

C

D

E

Chapter 6
Hitting Adaptions

At this point we have finished discussion on the hitting theories. Further understanding of the principles, and new knowledge, can be gained through an examination of the following stroke adaptions:

1. Adjustment to the inside pitch from the outside pitch approach.
2. Left-handed versus right-handed hitting.
3. Switch hitting.

As with much of the information in this book, this discussion is newly tapped hitting knowledge and information. However, advanced as it might be, I feel that discussion of these facets are paramount to the understanding of hitting a baseball.

ADJUSTMENT TO INSIDE PITCH
FROM AN OUTSIDE APPROACH

Recall once again **Charlie Lau's** words: "Gear yourself to the ball away and let the inside pitch take care of itself." This is but one of Lau's brilliant teachings which requires a closer look. He's talking about covering the middle and outside part of the plate and still hitting the inside pitch effectively—the hallmark of great hitting. Because of the importance of these concepts, and the difficulty of word descriptions, proceed slowly.

The hitter is concerned with plate coverage. To cover the plate, the good hitters gear their mechanics somewhere over the outer two thirds of home plate. This is because 80 percent of the pitches are thrown away from the hitter. This approach allows the hitter more time to accept the pitch. It also keeps the front shoulder and head in good hitting position. The stride is taken with the hips blocked off by the closed front foot. This keeps the hip structure closed, ready to attack the outside pitch. If the pitch is inside, a split-second, on-the-spot adjustment is made by: 1) pushing against the rigid front leg and utilizing more of the available hip rotation; 2) pivoting the front foot open to unblock the hips; 3) pulling the bat in and down with the bottom arm and; 4) switching to rear arm dominance from front arm dominance, which pushes the swing down through the ball with the top hand.

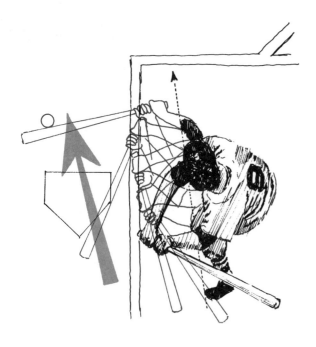

Body movements are initially directed to the outside half of the plate.

Inside pitch: front leg repels weight shift, arms pull in and top hand pushes forward.

Adjustments to inside pitch from an outside approach.

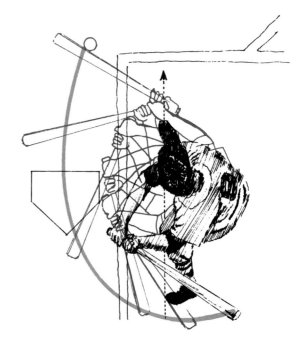

Great hitters are able to make this subtle adjustment *after striding into the pitch*. For the pitch over the outside half of the plate, the front leg accepts the weight and allows the swing to continue to the outside pitch. The front arm takes responsibility for guiding the bat to that area. The front arm and weight shift work in tandem.

For the inside pitch, the front leg firms, holds its angle and repels the weight shift, allowing the hips to pivot. The front arm pulls the bat in. The rear arm then takes over dominance to lead the hips around the front leg in rotation and contour the swing into a tighter arc.

Ideally, you want to be a weight shift hitter on the low and away pitch, a rotation hitter on the inside or high pitch, and a hybrid on the pitch down the middle.

Key: Stay smooth and relaxed when the tendency is to tighten up; quickness comes from relaxation, and you need to be quick inside.

Remember the words of **Al Kaline**: "I used to guide pretty much with my bottom hand and use my top hand when I wanted to generate power and quickness to the ball." Thus, the hitter "glides" to the outside or middle part, and "brakes" and switches to top hand on the inside half.

This shifting from weight shift/front arm pull to rotation/top hand push operates by a sixth sense which becomes instinctive. It can only be described by: "Gear yourself to the ball away and let the inside pitch take care of itself." This instinctive action can be acquired with much work, but it is an action the hitter can teach himself.

I found that when I was in a good streak I was reacting properly to the inside pitches. Getting jammed a couple of times may lead to an insecure feeling about your quickness. When you doubt your quickness inside you will go into a period of opening up your front side too quickly, which leads directly to a slump (see Chapter 3, "Keep the Front Side Closed"). Relax, stay smooth, and push the bat down through the ball.

LEFT-HANDED HITTING VERSUS RIGHT-HANDED HITTING

I have already touched upon some of the differences between left-handed and right-handed hitting. Erroneously, hitting principles have always been regarded as the same for hitters from both sides of the plate. But they are not the same.

The telltale clue is that left-handed hitters have infinitely more trouble hitting left-handed pitching than right-handers do right-handed pitching. A common explanation for this has been that left-handed hitters don't see that many left-handers. Bunk. Neither do right-handers. The problem is that left-handed hitters, facing so many opposite-handed pitchers (which requires less time to react) get lulled into using "front side" mechanics which can make for a slower swing. If the mechanics of hitting were the same for both hitters, both would hit "like-handed" (righty-righty, lefty-lefty) pitchers equally. But left-handers struggle more. Realizing why illuminates much hitting knowledge.

Both left-handed and right-handed hitters face different factors which require mechanical differences.

The variables responsible for mechanical differences in left-handed and right-handed hitters involve: 1) the hitter's *vision* of the pitcher's release, and; 2) the ball's *angle of flight* to the hitter.

Variable #1: Vision: The Angle of Release

Recognition of the type of pitch (curve, slider, fast ball) involves reading different *release angles* from the right- and left-handed pitchers. (Consult Lesson 3, "Vision".) The "like-handed" pitcher is more difficult to read because of the more acute angle of vision, which disguises the release angle.

Al Kaline: "You see the ball a little longer from the opposite hand thrower."

Al's right. And when the like-handed pitcher's arm action drops lower toward sidearm, the angle becomes even more acute and the pitch recognition more difficult.

Thus, the like-handed hitter must wait a split second *longer* to read the pitch from the like-handed pitcher. In taking more time to read the pitch he cannot use a lot of front side, slow bat characteristics. To wait the extra millisecond on the breaking ball, the like-handed hitter must use fast-bat characteristics.

There is another reason for the like-handed hitter using fast bat characteristics. There is always a millisecond of fear in the like-handed hitter when identifying a like-handed pitch. He must hold his ground in the launch position, keep his weight back, judge the pitch, and then strike. He can't use slow bat characteristics if he does this.

Variable #2: The Angle of Flight

Next, to hit the ball moving on an angle *away* from the hitter, as with all like-handed breaking pitches, the hitter must get the bat farther out in front of this pitch to hit it into fair territory, which means his swing must be quicker. For all of these reasons, hitting the like-hander will require quicker *rotational* characteristics—hip rotation, hitting against the front leg rather than over it, close hands, a level cut, a stroke with "pushing" characteristics. These mechanics will speed up the bat and give him more time to judge the pitch. Slow bat characteristics are eaten alive by the like-handed pitcher.

Left-handed hitters fall into the trap of slow bat characteristics because, growing up, there are significantly fewer left-handed pitchers to teach them they'd better be quicker. Even in pro baseball, left-handed pitchers are sometimes rare. Facing more right-handed pitchers (opposite throwers) allows the left-handed hitter to get away with a slower swing. The right-handed hitter, because he faces more right-handed pitchers (like-handers), is forced by Darwinian principle to evolve into more of a rotation hitter. If the situation was reversed, the right-handed hitter would evolve into the "lazy" hitter and the left-handed hitter would use more rotation.

This explains why the overwhelming majority of weight shift instructors are left-handed hitters—Waner, Walker, Moses, Lau, Hriniak, Carew, Pinson—and why left-handed hitters are their most effective disciples. It is also why many right-handed hitters struggle with weight shift. This is not to say that successful right-handed hitters have not used weight shift characteristics, just that they are exceptions. Roberto Clemente was a near perfect weight shift hitter. Harvey Kuenn, a pure weight shift hitter, won a batting title in the fifties and was a lifetime .300 hitter. Dick Groat won a batting championship with it. Aaron used some weight shift characteristics, although his top hand dominated his swing. But for the most part, right-handed weight shift hitters are generally platoon players, resting against right-handed pitchers because of difficulty with the inside fast ball/curve ball combination, which requires much quickness from the hitter. Weight shift characteristics tone down the adverse effects of pulling the ball, but the restriction of hip rotation and front arm emphasis render it more difficult to succeed from the right side where the hitter must be quicker a majority of the time.

This is why left-handed pitchers were no trouble for Ted Williams. He used rotational characteristics. Find me any left-handed hitter who hits lefties well and I'll show you his rotation/top hand features. Show me a hitter who struggles against the like-hander and I'll show you his weight shift features.

Ideally, the Weight Shift System is for the fleet left-handed hitter with no power. He makes more contact, more center and opposite field contact, and gets a great jump out of the box. The problems he'll have with left-handed pitchers can be worked through with his speed, and he can work on his bunting game as a defense against left-handers. The Combination System is ideal for the strong, slow-footed right-handed power hitter who is geared for the center of the plate because he can use it to defend against the right-handed pitcher's fast ball-in/breaking ball-away strategy. His jump out of the box can be sacrificed. He can use the same style against the left-handed pitcher, perhaps going for the long ball. Bob Watson, Joe Torre, and Richie Zisk are three fine examples.

SWITCH HITTING

One would think that, ideally, switch hitting would be the way to go. And ideally, it is. But ideals have a way of breaking down on practical application. A batter must know the pitfalls before investing hundreds of hours of work in attempting to hit from both sides of the plate.

The first problem is that, like the leisure pilot who upgrades to a two-engine airplane from a single-engine, he has doubled his chances for peril. The switch hitter must fine tune *two different* batting styles, when each one requires his utmost attention. As one old pro said to a rookie aspiring to switch hit, "Forget it, kid. Learn to lay off the breaking ball."

Learning to switch hit is worth the effort for the speedy, right-handed hitter who wants the closer jump out of the box from the left side. But for the hitter with some power, the pitfalls become pronounced.

The natural right-hander who moves over to the left side now has his dominant arm on the front side of the body, which also becomes the bottom hand on the bat—anatomical *and* physical law disadvantages. As a result, he pulls the bat through with the front arm and the front side, loses the top hand force, and severely compromises his power. These are not necessarily precursors to failure, however. The slower swing which results is used effectively by a fair portion of right hand-dominant left-handed hitters, although usually they have been at it since age six or so.

Al Kaline: "Switch hitting has to be something a hitter does when he's very, very young. I'm talking about a seven, eight, nine, ten years old—about the same time he's learning to hit. Very seldom do you see anyone pick it up after they've entered pro ball."

Worse, the new switch hitter will be forced to bat left-handed a *majority* of times, since most pitchers at all levels are right-handed. It is not horribly rare to see a good right-handed hitter take up switch hitting, become relatively proficient, and then lose his right-handed skills to infrequent right-handed plate appearances and become strictly a left-handed hitter.

Let me tell you what happened to me when I took up switch hitting during my freshman year in high school. The curve ball was killing me, so in desperation I tried to switch hit. I kept it up with little success and power from high school through my sophomore year in college. I almost felt better at least swinging hard and missing the curve than feebly swinging at the fast ball as a new lefty. In a game against Miami of Ohio I finally said the heck with it and stayed right-handed against a right-handed pitcher. I hit a home run and never switch hit again. Here's what it all amounted to: I spent most of my time hitting left-handed and my natural stroke stopped developing. My power was more than cut in half. I finally made up my mind to learn how to hit the curve ball. I'm thankful to have hit that home run against Miami, which opened up my eyes. Kind of like Darren Daulton finally directing his power to center. My eyes were opened up to a new concept and I began seeing things differently.

No one is saying switch hitting cannot be done, and be done to much improvement both to the team and the individual. Try it if you like. You may increase your production twofold. But given these drawbacks, switch hitting cannot be considered any sort of panacea or old equalizer to the breaking ball. If it were, everyone would turn around and the great ones like Wilson and Hornsby would have no doubt employed it. Given these pitfalls of switch hitting, it is almost as though the gods of baseball are saying, "Be thankful, son, for being able to hit one way. Work at it and perfect it. Do not look for shortcuts to success in this game."

Chapter 7
The Role of the Hitting Instructor

The hitting instructor should not be confined to his title, because the needs of his players go far beyond knowledge and skills with the bat. For example, it is known that Charlie Lau, one of the best, was first a common man's psychologist and was able to impart encouragement and curiosity to his pupils, then slip in something important. In other words, he established a *relationship* first, which opened the door to knowledge.

From my years in the game, two things have come very clear. First, players crave knowledge instinctively, and second, as long as they are playing and thinking baseball, knowledge is in the air. Much of it they will get themselves, if they are allowed to remain curious and open. The knowledge will come to them by osmosis, if in no other way. Therefore, a hitting coach can be effective, regardless of his knowledge of hitting, if he can keep the player's hopes and curiosity alive. This should be the first skill of a hitting instructor.

Often, a hitting instructor will be dealing with hitting problems which are not clear-cut. The hitter may be doubting himself, confused, or mired in a deep slump. He may believe in faulty mechanics. He will be searching for the magic solution of which no hitting instructor has total command. The solutions are often trial-and-error, hit-and-miss, until the hitter has what he needs. Your job as a coach is to keep this hitter going, searching, working, *often from nothing,* until spontaneously, he finds what he needs. In these cases, offer your best idea, maybe a drill tailored just for him, and in time he will find what he needs. In these cases, you start with nothing but the kindling of encouragement and offer a spark. The hitter will do his part when he has hope.

Just as likely, your knowledge will hold a key. *Join the player in his problem.* Talk as if it is your problem. Do this and you have jumped from hitting critic to hitting instructor. Analyze his problem along with him and give him your best solution. If you have studied with empathy, you will be correct more times than not.

Apply the principles you have learned, and structure a *simple* course of action. Demonstrate where you can, collect and use pictures to show what you mean. You plant a seedling, and support it with stakes and cords. Before the roots take hold, the wind may blow it away. You have no choice but to re-plant, re-stake.

Then, too, a hitting coach can be quite effective without a broad base of knowledge. Remember that a hitter needs to be reminded more than he needs to be instructed—to locate release points, to wait on the ball, to use his hands, to stay aggressive when the count is in his favor, to choke up with two strikes. The real job of every hitting instructor is to keep bringing the hitter back, time after time, to the old simple principles which he has gotten away from, to the work habits, to the tiresome challenge of facing opponent after opponent.

Avoid drenching the hitter with large amounts of knowledge. Do not coach him with an idea of showing him how smart you are, or you will come out dumb. And remember, the whole bottle of medicine cannot be taken in one day. Dispense it in daily doses, careful not to get ahead of schedule. Allow the infirmity to be replaced by health in gradual improvements.

In the case of mechanical adjustments, I have found it best to have the hitter experience the new action in slow motion first, followed by dry swing work. Let him get the *feel* first. Make sure he memorizes this feel with his muscles. Then use dry swings, tee work, toss-ups, and batting practice, in that order. Breakdown at any level calls for a retreat to the previous one. Repetition is the key.

For mental mechanics, almost endless, well-timed reminders designed to gently nudge the idea home is effective. Voice your reminders in different ways, with different terminology meaning the same thing, one principle at a time. Learn to say the same thing using different words, different terms. Some terms mean different things to different hitters.

Psychological principles teach that immediate correction is best, but *not so* in teaching baseball skills. Leave the player's hitting mistakes alone *during* the game. After he makes an out, he is hurting. The hitter will be too upset, too angry to accept criticism, no matter how well intended. Worse, not only will he be unable to hear you, he may build up resentment at the timing of your teaching. During the game he is ripe to take your comments as *punishment*, and coaching should never be taken as punishment. During the game is the time to encourage him. Unless it is a mental reminder, save your comments on mechanics until after the game, when the equipment is in the bag. At this time do not condemn, but offer your coaching as something to work on, something to think about, something that will help in the future. Never bludgeon the player with advice, always offer it as a pillow.

"YOUR BAT HAS A HOLE IN IT..."

The best coaching tip I ever received was this: *smile* when you are coaching a player individually. If you cannot smile, withhold your ideas until you can.

Another good rule is: never criticize or point out fault unless you have an idea to make it better. This way you are not just bringing bad news. This encourages the hitter by giving him something to work with.

Above all, use your common sense in acquiring teaching knowledge. Instruction is everywhere, and not all of it is good. A lot of hitting instruction is contradictory. Examine it on its merit according to face value evidence and common sense before imparting it to a player. The Hippocratic Oath applies to teaching baseball as well as it does to medicine. "Do thy patient no harm."

Bob Watson: "I think the best hitting coach in the world is the guy who can take what the young man has and get him to do the best he can with that. Not to try to clone him to hit one specific way or another, but to be what he is. Now if he proves to you he can't get it done that way, then make some subtle changes, not whole scale changes. If he needs changing, shape him away from what he is, slowly, toward what may work better. A total makeover is not what a player needs at any age."

Hard work, perseverance, patience, and basic knowledge is standard with the professional hitting instructor. At the professional level the instructor must have a sense of what goes through a hitter's mind during the game, and the ability to influence the hitter's *thinking* during the game. Show me a hitting coach who can affect a game in progress with a suggestion he makes to a hitter and that guy's someone special.

Part Two:
The Combined System Hitting Skills and Technique

A) *Eyes locked on contact zone.*
B) *Bat in level path to ball.*
C) *Front leg accepts the weight shift with angled front leg.*
D) *Contact with ball in the two to four-o'clock "time zone".*
E) *Ideal contact zone between toe of striding foot and center line of body. (This will occur over home plate if the toe strides to the front edge of home plate.)*
F) *Striding foot closed.*
G) *Level hip rotation.*
H) *Level shoulder rotation.*
I) *Top arm in the process of extension on contact.*

Lesson 1:
Pulling Versus Square Contact

I f a hitter asked the question, "Word for word, what is the most important thing a hitter can know?", this lesson would contain his answer. This lesson concerns the pivotal issue of "pulling" the ball to one's power field versus striving for square, center field contact. This addresses his questions of where, when, and how to hit the baseball.

In Hitting Theory we explored the systems of hitting movement designed to effectively deliver the bat to the point of contact with quickness, consistency, and power. The Lau method is clearly geared for square, straight away, center field contact, and it has some built-in adjustments for pulling the ball when applicable. The Williams method is clearly more conducive to pulling the pitch to the power field. This in mind, some universal statements can be made about pulling versus striving for square, center field contact.

For the purpose of illustration, let's assume a bat has seven inches of good, firm hitting resistance on the barrel. As the bat angle required to pull the ball to the power field increases, this hitting surface decreases.

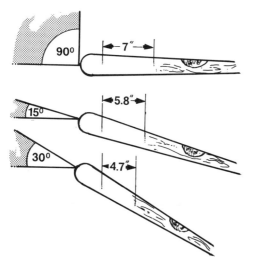

As the bat gets further out in front the prime hitting surface shrinks.

Harry Walker: "When hitting straight away, the surface of the bat is so much bigger. When you're pulling, the bat is at such an angle that you have to be so accurate, so precise. Your timing crucial. When hitting straight away you can be a little quick or a little late and still hit the ball sharply. To pull it, your timing needs to be perfect."

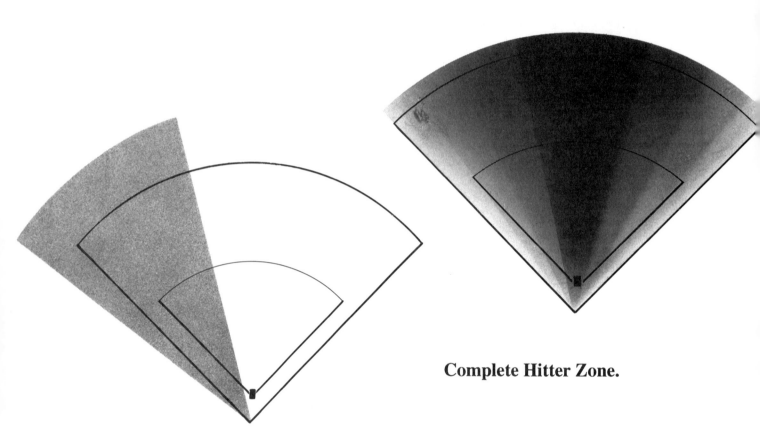

Complete Hitter Zone.

Right-handed Pull Hitter Zone.

In addition, the pull hitter is easy to pitch to. He is openly vulnerable to off-speed pitches. The hitter who uses all fields is difficult for a pitcher to pitch to. He's a more complete hitter, less vulnerable to the pitcher's tricks.

Of course, pulling the ball is the shortest route to home run territory. It makes sense that the fences will give the hitter a "break" in distance if the hitter can successfully pull the ball. A well-stroked, pulled ball is an admirable feat, but rather than allowing this to become the goal, many contact hitters consider this to be a lucky mistake. The mistake is being too quick.

Pulling the ball to the power field requires:
1. More quickness, bringing in the urge to start too soon.
2. More precise hand-eye coordination because the angle of the bat reduces hitting surface.
3. More timing accuracy because of the reduced hitting surface.

Conversely, it can be said that square contact requires:
1. Less quickness, allowing the luxury of waiting on the pitch.
2. Less precise hand-eye coordination because of the increased hitting surface.
3. Less timing accuracy.

Carrying point 3 above one step further, if the straight away hitter is a hair late or early, good contact is still probable. However, if the pull hitter is a hair late or early, contact is adversely effected.

Listen to **Harry Walker:** "In order to pull the ball, you've got to be so quick that you'll have to cheat a little bit, and every time they throw a change up or breaking ball, you're going to be too far out in front. And this is what gets a lot of hitters. If you watch the big league hitters, as good as they are, they get in the habit of doing this. When they start soon like this they chase a lot of bad balls, where if they're waiting they'd take that pitch. This waiting, I think, is the secret in hitting.

"If I can't wait without cheating a lot [starting too quick] and being fooled a lot on a change up or a breaking ball, then I should hit the fast ball back further, more toward the middle of the plate so that I have a little bit longer to look at the ball. The position of contact is *more over the plate*, which sends the pitch right back at the pitcher" (italics mine).

It should come as no surprise which type of hitting batting champions prefer. **Walker:** "Nearly all hitters who have led the league except Ted Williams have been straight away, opposite field hitters. They use the gaps. Sixty-five to eighty percent of what they hit is straight away or to the opposite field. They wait and see what the ball is going to do before swinging."

This is precisely what I should have done in college to learn to hit the curve ball, which plagued me from an early age. This whole field concept was what I began to use in 1974, after I hit just .196 in 1973. I loved watching Roberto Clemente hit when I was a boy. I'd seen him play in Cincinnati and then later when I was with the Phillies. His whole hitting system seemed to take aim on the right-center field gap. He was a good high ball hitter, and when he got one he really drove it to right center field. He'd pull the breaking ball and bash the fastball the other way. After the 1973 season I compared our styles. I hit one way, dead pull, and was struggling badly. He hit a different way, to the opposite field, and was very successful. He was hard to strike out, I was easy. The differences became crystal clear. I didn't want to sacrifice my power so I compromised our styles. I added some weight shift movement and began taking aim on center field. I had to back off the plate and wait for the ball. I would have more things to learn yet, but that change got me going in the big leagues.

There are other reasons for wanting to see what the ball is going to do before swinging. If you can "wait," "recognize," and "lay off" bad pitches or pitcher's pitches, you can work more counts in your favor. I always felt that the most important step in learning to wait is developing a "straight away" stroke. Don't look to pull the ball, pull only by accident. Do what Walker is telling you. Set your sights up the middle. You do this by waiting longer.

If you still have trouble waiting, visualize a line drive at the first baseman's knees (third baseman for a lefty). Thinking like this will calibrate your timing back, and you can literally pick the fast ball out of the catcher's mitt if your swing is level.

Lesson 2:
The Contact Zone

In order to hit the ball in the Complete Hitter Zone consistently, the majority of contact will not occur out in front of the plate. It will occur *over* the plate.

Nearly everyone agrees that hitting the ball hard to center field is good hitting. Do you know that it is impossible to hit the ball *hard* to center field if contact is made in front of home plate? (Assuming the hitter is not standing in front of the box, he will have to reach.) He hits the ball hard to center field by hitting the ball over the front half of home plate. And to hit the ball over the plate, the arms cannot fully extend forward.

A hitter makes several discoveries when he plays as long as I did. One of my major ones didn't come until 1979, seven years into my career. What was it? I learned how to wait longer on the pitch. In order to wait longer, you have to *create* more time. After a life of dead pull hitting, strike outs, and home runs, rather one-dimensional hitting, I decided to *back off from the plate* and *stand deeper in the box*, like George Brett was doing in Kansas City. This gave me the freedom to wait longer, hit the ball over the plate, more specifically between the center line of my body and the toe of my striding foot, and effectively use the entire field. More important, I was free to extend my arms on all pitches without having to hit them out in front of the plate. That year I hit 45 home runs. From then on I was no longer a one-dimensional, feast or famine type hitter. As proof, the following two years were my MVP years. The pieces were coming together. Of course, **Harry Walker** was saying this stuff twenty, thirty years before. I believe the chain went something like this: Somebody, maybe Waner, gave it to Walker. Walker gave it Lau, Lau gave it to Brett, Brett gave it to me. I don't need it any longer. I'm giving it to you.

Harry Walker: "The vast majority of hitters who have led the league hit the ball more straight away, more over the plate. They wait and see what the ball is going to do."

To get what Walker is talking about, think of contact as being made in a two-to-four o'clock contact zone for the right-handed hitter, and eight-to-ten o'clock left-handed time.

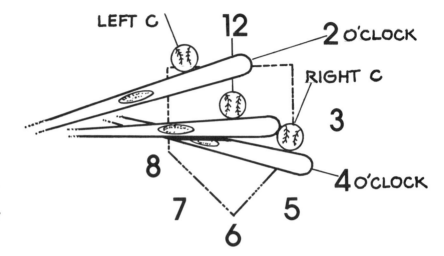

The bat makes contact in the two to four o' clock contact zone (eight to ten o'clock left-handed time), not in the one o'clock position in front of the plate (eleven o'clock left-handed time.)

Position yourself in the batter's box so that the end of your stride stops even with the front edge of home plate. Now *push* your bat from the side into the two-to-four o'clock bat position (eight-to-ten o'clock left-handed time). You will find that this is the area of ideal, square contact, if you are pushing with the rear arm. Adjust your foot position so that the barrel of your bat is in this zone where your arms are half to three-quarters of full extension. Trying to hit the ball farther out in front of the plate than this will force you to start your swing too soon, and you will be fooled more often.

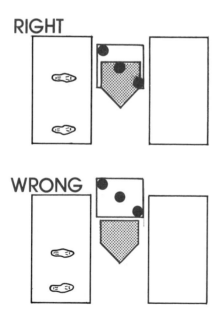

RIGHT

WRONG

For maximum contact thrust, the ball is struck while the arms and bat are *in the process of extension*. Full extension occurs after the ball has left the bat. Even the boxer knocks out his man before his arm is extended. *Full extension with locked out arms is follow-through action only.*

This is not to say that you will never hit the ball out in front of the plate. You will. When it happens, you'll take it. But the price of *striving* to hit the ball out in front of the plate is a big one—the hitter gives up his ability to wait on the breaking ball. Another reason not to make your goal of hitting the ball out in front with extended arms: it doesn't happen that often. If you're waiting to see the pitch, there just aren't that many opportunities. How many 500-foot home runs did Mantle hit in his career? Ten, twenty? That's ideal, in-front-of-the-plate contact. And that's about how often it happens.

Richie Zisk: "The balls that I really drove to right center, balls I hit out of the park, those balls got deeper into my zone. In other words, I didn't go out and get it."

The number one problem among young hitters (and some older ones as well) is hitting the curve ball. Much of this is due to their belief in hitting the pitch out in front of the plate. To do this, they have to start the swing too early so when the curve ball comes up, they haven't got a chance. To hit the breaking ball, you've got to wait long enough to see if and where it will break. This requires time and rules out trying to pull the fast ball.

Al Kaline: "The breaking ball will always give the hitter problems if he's got his mind on pulling the ball. This happens less to the player set up to hit the ball straight away. He tends to keep his head on the ball more, his shoulder in."

Say a hitter is waiting for the break on the curve ball, looking out over the plate (middle to outside half). What if the inside fast ball comes up? *Take it*. **Kaline**: "The hitter should take that pitch, unless he has two strikes. If he has two strikes, he does what he can."

Coaches: when you tell a young player to hit the ball in front of the plate, he thinks one o'clock contact (eleven o'clock left-handed time.) He thinks you are telling him to pull the ball. This is misleading and erroneous. **Walker** has it right:

Harry Walker: "Most hitters, at least seventy-five percent of them, would be better off if they hit the ball more over the plate, straight away, rather than pulling out and trying to hit the ball out in front of the plate. When a hitter goes into a slump, nine out of ten times that is what he is doing. Only if the hitter has power should he try to be quick enough to hit the ball in front of the plate and pull out [his front side]."

One last point about hitting the ball further back in the strike zone. Have you ever noticed how the pepper hitter always gets a piece of the ball? You can never fool him. Throw him a curve ball, fast ball, slider, or change-of-pace, and he'll have no problem. I've been in pepper games where pro pitchers are throwing nearly their best stuff and the hitter always gets a piece of the ball. We need to ask ourselves why. The answer is obvious. *Because he doesn't try to hit the ball out in front of the plate.* He waits for the ball to come to him and makes square, center field contact over the plate. He pushes out the inside pitch and centers the rest. He is hitting the way **Harry Walker** recommends hitting. Waiting as he does, *he can't get fooled.* If the object of pepper was to *pull* the ball, he would be fooled as easily as the hitter at home plate. We can learn from this.

When a hitter tries to make contact out in front of the plate, he has to start his bat too soon. When he starts his bat too soon, he gets fooled.

In summary, extension over the plate, not in front of it, should be the optimum goal of each swing. Extension cannot always be achieved, especially when the hitter is behind in the count. When ahead in the count the hitter should look to extend on balls out over the plate and "take" the inside strike, where he won't have enough time to extend.

Remember, extension over the plate, not in front of it.

Drills

1. Pepper. As you play, notice where contact is made in relation to a home plate.

2. Tee work in the two-to-four o'clock zone, eight-to-ten o'clock left-handed time. Remember to "swing-press" with the hands. Do not worry if the ball does not seem to jump off the bat. In a game, the velocity of the pitch meeting the mass of the bat provides the power. Square contact with the barrel of the bat is what this game is about.

3. Place the tee out in front of home plate. Now try hitting to center field. You will find yourself reaching.

Lesson 3:
Hand Action

HANDS START THE STROKE

In contrast to the golfer, the hitter must strike instantaneously, some-times when his mechanics are out of sequence. Because the pitcher's goal is to upset timing, the hitter will sometimes have to strike when the pitch is *almost by him*, other times when his weight shift happens ahead of a slow pitch. If the front side and the lead arm start the swing, as they do in golf, the swing can be too slow, because of the delayed action in getting the movement to the bat. *Timing problems are corrected by fast hands which make up the difference of unsynchronized mechanics.*

Hand speed means nothing in golf because the ball is stationary, so the golfer employs the front side and lead arm for accuracy. He can even stop his swing and start over if he wants to. But to the hitter, hand speed is everything because the pitch is traveling at high speed in unpredictable ways and sometimes you *have* to swing.

Richie Zisk on hands: "You can make a lot of mistakes with your body, your hips, and your shoulders, but if you have good quick hands and keep them back, you can make up for a lot of that. On the other hand, you can have everything else mechanically correct but if you've got poor hand speed, you're in a world of trouble."

The hitter will go a long way when he realizes that his hand speed is vital in governing the *start, delay, speed, and direction* of his stroke. The third key on **Rod Carew's** list of ten keys to good hitting is: "Use your hands. Become an aggressive hands hitter. This allows you to wait longer on the pitch and react to changes in pitch direction."

Building the skill of hand quickness is as easy as switching on a light. First, understand that hand speed is a *physical concept*. The body must become *aware* of how the hand and wrist muscles should work. You can get this concept by taking your stance and *feel only the power in your hands, your grip*. Let nothing else register. Grip the bat firmly at the "pad" of the hand located at the base of the fingers, not back in the palm. Squeeze and release the handle of your bat with your fingers to burn in the feel of strength. Now start your swing with your hands *only*, starting your hands from the launching position. Again, *hands only*. You'll find that the other body parts, particularly the hip rotation, fall in line *automatically*. Once you have the feel in your hands, never lose it. Rehearse it as much as you can.

If you give a ball bat to a five-year-old and tell him to swing it, he'll swing it with his entire body because he doesn't yet have strength in his hands. He will tend to accelerate the bat over a long arc to get decent bat speed. He will use his front side to pull it through, often to the point of lunging, much like the old-timer whose bat was measured in pounds rather than ounces. Too often this habit never leaves him, as though it imprints forever. It is not uncommon to see 200 pound men still doing the same thing. This has nothing to do with strength. They never converted away from using the front side and the front shoulder to the hands.

On the other hand, I once saw an 11-year-old girl use her hands as well as a professional player. I was pitching to her team in a clinic. When she walked to the plate, all the other girls ran to the outfield fence, screaming. I couldn't figure out why. When the balls began jumping off her bat, I knew. Somehow she had gotten the physical concept of using her hands, which had nothing to do with strength. Who knows, maybe her mom taught it to her.

In his book, *The Art of Hitting .300,* **Charlie Lau** says, "The hitter must step first and swing second. Players who combine the two actions invariably . . . start swinging the bat at the same time they are striding. This reduces both their power and their ability to make contact with the ball."

From Lau's insistence on the separation of stride and swing, this seems to be clear evidence that hands work independently of the body. And, once the striding action is taken, the hands initiate the swing on their own. Thus, from the launching position it's "hands first." Try it.

One point will help you in your hand work. You're in the launching position. Say you decide to take the pitch. Your hands should never move forward. If they do, your arms are pulling the bat. You're not using your hands!

One other **Lau** gem requires our attention. He said, "You've got to plan to swing at every pitch." He means that all hitting actions are geared to execute on every delivery. As the trigger of swing execution, the hands determine if the swing continues after the stride or not. This triggering action by the hands is all-or-nothing, one hundred percent or zero.

Drills

1. Take your stance in a quiet room. Swing the bat. Listen to the sound, the *hum*, it makes traveling through the air. Now, focusing on the hands, swing faster. Listen to the noise. Now faster yet, and listen. Faster yet, using your hands, wrists, *and elbows*. Faster. Tighten the arc. Make the hum into a *roar* by adding a little hip rotation.

2. Repeat the same drill with a friend. See who can make the most "noise." Be careful not to hit any lamps!

3. Swing the bat with the *hands only*, nothing else. No stride, just the hands. Begin by *twisting the bat from the launching position in the stance all the way into follow-through.* Allow the body to pivot freely *but do not consciously pivot. Let the hands and bat swing the body.* You will see that the hands start the swing and everything else falls in line *with them.*

   If you can add your stride and hip rotation to the hand action, you've got it.

   Tip: You will also notice that a firm grip is required to start the bat from the launching position.

4. Place the ball on the batting tee so that the two seams are vertical and face behind toward the catcher. As you swing, hit the inside seam. This demonstrates the push element of the swing. Feel it. Also, note where the ball is placed in relation to home plate for the best results.

KEEP THE BAT ABOVE FOREARM LEVEL
"Barrel Above the Hands"

The force of the top hand connot work unless the bat is in favorable position to accept it. For top hand force to be effective, the bat cannot dip below "forearm level". "Forearm level" can be defined as a line passing from the elbow through the hand. Both bones in the lower arm are part of the line. When the bat head dips below this line, the hands stop working and the front side takes over, slowing down bat velocity. The same thing would occur if you were pounding a nail and the hammer angle went below forearm level.

Bat should remain above forearm level throughout the swing.

Bats dipping below forearm level.

Proper use of the hands from the launching position, a flat bat angle, and level shoulder rotation will keep the barrel above the hands and forearm level.

KEEP THE FRONT SIDE CLOSED UNTIL THE HANDS BEGIN WORKING

In the stance the front shoulder is pointed at the pitcher, resting beneath the chin. The front side of the body faces 90 degrees away from the pitcher. After the striding foot lands the hands begin working by tightening up their linkage to the body with firm pressure, and then begin pushing the bat into the swing arc. At this point, the front side (belt buckle) begins its 90 degree turn toward the pitcher. Remember, any premature movement toward the pitcher, a false start or flinch by the hands, will incorrectly allow the front shoulder to open. This is why hand work is vital. Hands must stay back!

Frank Howard: "Lock up that front side until the hands begin working."

Exactly. Hands first, front side second.

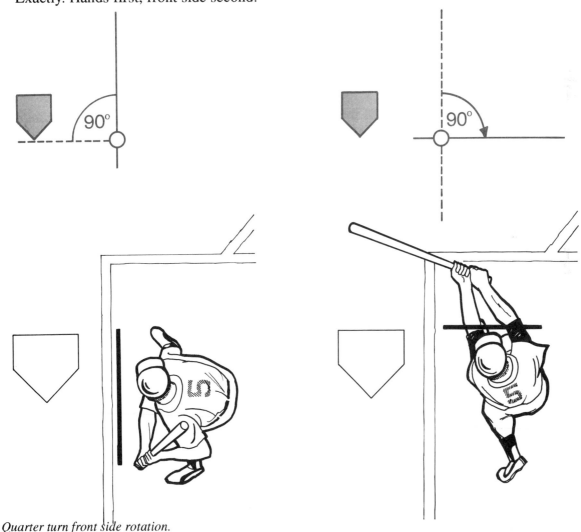

Quarter turn front side rotation.

More **Frank Howard** on keeping the front side closed: "I like to use the expression 'we have a fast hip [front side opening] action, but it's a late action.' This makes it a snap. If I open the hips [and front shoulder] too soon, the front side is going to fly open and I'll lose my power."

Al Kaline: "My secret was to always keep that front shoulder closed until the last instant. That way my hands had to start. This way I could still handle the outside pitch but keep everything together to rotate my hips and get my hands through on the inside pitch."

Clarence Jones: "Hitters sometimes hurry their feet [knee cock, stride, landing, resulting in premature hip turn] and you have to slow them down. When a hitter hurries his feet, his actions happen too fast and he'll drag the bat. Slow his feet down. Slow feet [deliberate, relaxed movement] results in quick hands."

NOTE: Compare **Howard's** statement with that from **Jones**: **Howard:** "If I open the hips [and front shoulder] too soon, the front side is going to fly open and I'll lose my power." **Jones:** "When a hitter hurries his feet, his actions happen too fast and he'll drag the bat."

These men are saying the same thing. Combined, they read like this: "When a hitter hurries his actions, the front side opens up too soon and upsets the rhythm of the swing. The power is lost and the bat drags because the hands cannot work."

Remember, all hitting movements except the hands and hips are slow, steady, relaxed, fluid. Keeping the front side closed is vital. If **Al Kaline** calls it his secret we'd do well to label it top priority.

To capsulize, there are two kinds of swings. One is pulled through by the front arm and front shoulder, which tends to restrict hip rotation (review Front Arm Versus Rear Arm in "Five Hitting Principles.) The other type of swing is dominated by the hand snap, using both hands. The second is by far the quicker, and facilitates hip rotation.

Lesson 4:
Pre-swing Actions

"Hitting is a lot like dancing. A hitter needs rhythm and movement not only with his bat but his body as well. I'm a big believer in rhythm, hip rock, the hitter getting and keeping himself in motion from the very beginning."
                                                    —Richie Zisk

COILING THE BODY

I like that description. There is a rhythm to hitting, a slow building motion, a sudden strike, and then a release. It is a rhythmic dance step that takes place with each pitch. If it helps, picture a cat preparing his body to pounce, or a snake coiling to strike. They're preparing their posture for sudden movement.

If I could point out one of my persistent hitting faults, and there were plenty over the years, it would be the inconsistency of my pre-swing movement. Yes, I did rock my hips naturally to the rhythm of the delivery, but my hands, stride, and upper body trended to fall forward into the ball instead of striding lightly with my weight back. I was getting into the pitch too quickly. I wasn't dancing lightly, I was charging.

Like me, if you need work in your pre-swing movement, remember **Charlie Lau's** words, "You've got to go back before you can go forward."

The ability to keep your weight back with a knee turn and a small hitch will increase bat speed and power. Some hitters have this sense naturally, others acquire it through fierce repetition. (The reader is asked to see "Mechanical Action" of the Lau Weight Shift Theory as a reference.)

Here is a sequence you can follow to correctly pick up this skill.

1. Put the bat down. Stand next to an imaginary plate as if you are facing a pitcher. Turn the front knee in four to ten inches and then put it back down in the same place. Feel the weight being transferred to the rear leg. Do this ten times using no stride.

2. Now repeat, only take your normal stride. Stride with your weight on the back leg, like you are striding cautiously into a puddle of water. Again, ten times.

3. Pick up the bat. Time a small twitch or hitch of the bat to the knee turn and put the foot down in the same place. Ten times.

4. Repeat step #3 but now use a stride. Ten times.

5. Repeat step #4 but now *swing the bat*. Remember to cock the hands with a small hitch or backward press into the launching position when you cock your knee. Ten times.

Repeat these steps ten more times, a hundred times, five hundred times, a thousand times, until the movement becomes natural. Do not perform these actions quickly or jerk into them. All hitting movements prior to the hand action are fluid, balanced, soft, flexible, deliberate. Only the hands are fast.

Clarence Jones: "Slow the feet [coiling action] down."

My axiom: "Slow feet, fast hands."

TIMING

A good rule of thumb for when to take the stride is when the ball passes the pitcher's head in his delivery, an instant *before* release. When the pitcher shows you his back pocket, the hitter should be rocking or coiling into the launch position. This would put the striding foot on the ground a split second *after* release. It means the cocking action of the hips, or knee turn, will occur as the pitcher brings the ball forward.

Timing takes much practice and precision. This is why it can take some big leaguers weeks of spring training to refine the delicate timing of their stride and mechanics.

The stride can be taken forward in time with the ball passing the pitcher's ear.

Billy Williams: "You let the pitcher do most of the work in your timing. When his hand starts to come forward toward the top of his motion, then I push my hands back four to six inches. They'd be like a bow and arrow, or a hammer on a gun, when they'd go back into the launching position." (For a review of hand momentum going into the launch position, see Chapter 4, Williams' Rotation Theory, "Mechanical Action.")

Key for the Advanced Hitter: Batting champions **Ted Williams** and **Joe Torre** "hit off the slider," or, they timed their stride and mechanics to the speed of the pitcher's slider. This is the "in-between" pitch as far as velocity is concerned. They felt that they could adjust with their hands up or down to the fast ball and curve. **Richie Zisk** and **Frank Robinson** hit off the fast ball and adjusted to the curve. **Mel Ott** and **Brooks Robinson** keyed off the breaking ball and adjusted upward to the fast ball. Generally, I would vary my strategy based on my knowledge of the pitcher's best pitch and the game situation. In the big leagues, the slider is the number one "out" pitch to the like-handed hitter (because it looks so much like a fast ball), and like Torre and Williams, I always "guarded" against the slider. However, there are a few pitchers that don't throw the slider, like Gooden, Glavine, and Ryan. Against these pitchers my timing was on their fast balls.

A precise hitter will experiment with his timing by "setting" it for different pitches. This is a truly fine sense, but good hitters work at the delicate process of adjusting their timing to different pitches and situations until they become great hitters.

VISION: Picking up the Pitch

Know *where* to look for the ball. If you can't see it, you'll never hit it. Finding the pitcher's point of release, seeing the ball come out of his hand, and knowing how each pitch *looks* coming out of the hand is a skill every hitter must have. Without this skill the best mechanics in baseball become useless.

So where should the hitter look? We suggest focusing on the pitcher's face as a starting point. The pitcher's face is not just a resting point for the eyes. Much can be learned from looking into a pitcher's eyes. His expression may show an array of emotion—apprehension, confidence, fear, doubt. He may shake off a sign tentatively, or agree with one confidently. This is information you can use when comparing it to his reaction after the pitch. And by staring at him you'll be offering a challenge, which is what it's all about anyway.

Billy Williams: "Sometimes it would seem like every pitcher was throwing ninety-five, 100 miles-per-hour, simply because I looked the pitcher in the face and I wouldn't go to the release point quick enough. I'd see the ball halfway to home plate and that's what makes a hitter jumpy, when he can't see things clearly."

When the pitcher's body pivots and his arm begins forward, your eyes can move to the release point. The hitter could fix his eyes elsewhere prior to release—shoulder, neck, or chest. But thinking about it a little, if the hitter can't stand looking into the eyes of his opponent he probably doesn't belong in the batter's box. Besides, the pitcher isn't looking at you. He's looking at the catcher.

Frank Robinson: "There is an area, a square somewhere next to each pitcher's head where he'll release the ball, and I will follow his hand up into that square and see the ball come out of that square. It will vary from pitcher to pitcher."

As the ball comes out of the pitcher's hand, recognition of the pitch begins. So many people say that the hitter sees the spin of the ball, the seams. I don't believe it. I couldn't. "Reading seams" to recognize the pitch is more of a myth. Great hitters talk about reading seams and then

a young hitter tries to do it and it's impossible. He gets discouraged and puts up his bat. The truth is that nobody has the eyes to read seams until the ball is on top of the hitter. Nobody has the eyesight to read seams rotating twenty feet out of the pitcher's hand, and the last ten feet is too late. This would mean a hitter "reads" seams for the middle thirty foot distance and reacts, something which happens for approximately one-fifth of a second. Hardly. Nerve impulses can't travel that fast. By the time the ball gets close enough to see seams, it's too late. The hitter recognizes the pitch from the *angle* it leaves the pitcher's hand, the pitcher's arm action, and by *initial thrust* out of the pitcher's hand.

The hitter's sight switches from the ball to the side of the head as the pitcher's arm comes forward. The hitter must know this area ahead of time because each pitcher has a different release point.

fast ball

slider (right handed)

curve ball

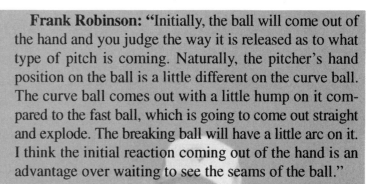

Frank Robinson: "Initially, the ball will come out of the hand and you judge the way it is released as to what type of pitch is coming. Naturally, the pitcher's hand position on the ball is a little different on the curve ball. The curve ball comes out with a little hump on it compared to the fast ball, which is going to come out straight and explode. The breaking ball will have a little arc on it. I think the initial reaction coming out of the hand is an advantage over waiting to see the seams of the ball."

The **fast ball** appears to leave the pitcher's hand on an immediate, but slight, *downward* angle. There is much *thrust* on the ball out of his hand.

The **slider** leaves the hand between these two angles with thrust. (To the like-handed hitter, the-low-and-away slider release appears nearly identical to the fast ball release. This is why it is so difficult to hit.)

The **curve ball** appears to leave the pitcher's hand on a slight upward and outward angle. It has a little hump on it. It does not explode out of the hand.

The **change-of-pace** release angle is identical to the fast ball, but has no thrust. (High change-of-paces are similar to curve ball releases, and are picked up quickly.)

The trained hitter knows the minute differences in these release angles. This allows him to hit the different pitches even in poorly lit ballparks where the ball appears seamless. Recognizing them, he will adjust his mechanics ever so slightly, but his hands remain *uncommitted* in the launching position until the decision to swing is made.

change up

Waiting for the Curve Ball

I must repeat. The decision on whether or not to swing is made in the launch position. The stride occurs at the same moment and in the same spot on every pitch, timed to the release of the ball. The pitcher's job is to get the hitter to commit his hands to the fast ball which will leave him no chance of hitting the off-speed pitches (curve ball). This is why it is crucial to keep the hands back when striding into the launch position. The best hitters are the ones who can keep their hands uncommitted until they recognize the angle of the pitch and decide to swing. In a nutshell, *waiting on the curve occurs in the launch position with hands back.* Hands that move prematurely forward are ineffective, weak, not used properly, and basically dead.

What happens when you are looking for a curve and a fast ball comes up? If you have mastered the push-swing element of the stroke, with the hands leading the way into the strike zone, you'll be able to recover. However, you will not be able to pull the pitch in all likelihood. Be satisfied with center and opposite field contact.

Drills

1. Stand in the bullpen batter's box against your own pitcher. Recognize where the pitcher's release angle comes from. Now stare at his face and switch to the release point as his arm begins coming forward. This is a "see only" drill. Do not swing.
2. Watch as many releases as you can, whether it is behind the bullpen or behind the screen. The pro has seen thousands of release angles by the time he gets to the major leagues. Watch both the right-handed release and the left-handed release. Vision will be better on the opposite-handed thrower because of the angle.

NOTE: Because of the line of sight to the like-hander's angle, his release angles are more difficult to decipher. Picking up these angles will take more practice.

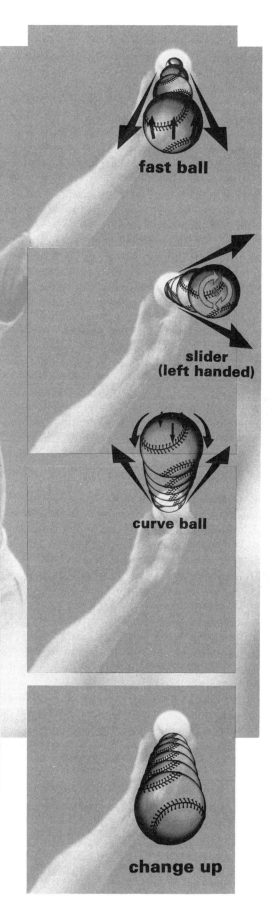

fast ball

slider (left handed)

curve ball

change up

Pete Rose showing level hip and shoulder rotation on the high pitch, and his bat completes the level arc.

Lesson 5: Physical Concepts

LEVEL BODY SEGMENT ROTATION

For maximum use of energy while swinging the bat, the force should be directed on a direct collision course with the pitch. The hips, shoulders, hands, and bat must direct their energy into the path of the pitch. This is done with level body segment rotation.

Also, level body segment rotation will keep the bat off the low pitch out of the strike zone.

The hitter who uses a jackknifed, crouched stance will get uneven shoulder rotation. This allows the whole shoulder assembly to rotate in an upward plane. This makes the rear shoulder dip and allows the arms to go lower into bad ball hitting area. Compare the last photo for shoulder rotation with my follow-through. My low finish means level shoulder rotation.

Drills

1. Structure your stance so that you are more vertical and not crouched deeply.

2. Dry swings (without a bat) in a mirror. Watch the plane of your bat. Is it direct, forward? Level?

3. Dry swings with your eyes closed. When your eyes are closed, your *internal eye* takes over. Feel the balance, rhythm, and direction of your force. Is it level?

4. Tee work. Have a teammate or coach watch from the side to see if your shoulders, hips, and bat are coming through on a level plane.

HITTING THE HIGH STRIKE

Pitchers are trained to throw low strikes. They get hurt less keeping the ball low. They are more successful when keeping the ball low. Hitters fail more chasing low pitches. Another reason low pitches are "pitcher's pitches": they are farther away from the eyes. The farther away from the eyes, the less accurate the hitter will be in centering the low pitch with his bat. This should tell the hitter something. It should tell the hitter that low pitches are pitcher's pitches. Conversely, high strikes are hitters' pitches. If you can get backspin on the high pitch with a tomahawking level cut, nothing can stop you. High pitches, hit like this, by any pitcher's admission, mean long hits—doubles, triples, and home runs.

No hitter can cover the entire strike zone effectively. Doesn't it make sense to cover the portion of the plate which the hitter not only sees better, but which will deliver the gap hits when he hits them on the nose? And if the hitter can program his stroke to a certain portion of the strike zone, shouldn't it be the "good" strikes?

As seen in the picture below, high strikes are from mid-thigh to the belt. This hitter is programming his swing to the high strike, with the bat maintaining an angle above forearm level. This keeps his swing off low pitches. The gray areas surrounding this zone represent borderline run-over close to this zone which the hitter can be expected to strike at from time to time.

If the hitter programs his stroke to a low zone, look where his borderline run-over goes. Pitchers make their living in this gray area. Great hitters learn this principle. Don't for one minute think that Aaron, Ruth, Greenberg, or Mays hit so many home runs swinging at low strikes. They programmed their swings to include pitches they could drive with backspin.

Al Kaline on patience and seeing the high strike: "I'd take the low pitch until I got two strikes and make him [the pitcher] get it up where I could see it a little better."

Billy Williams: "When you're ahead in the count, you look for a ball over the plate and up in the strike zone. These are the pitches we hit home runs off a long time ago. But it seems like hitters take these pitches now. They take them instead of looking for them. [Andre] Dawson will swing at that high pitch. Sandberg, too, but too often when the pitcher makes a mistake up, so many hitters will take it. When I played, guys like Mays would never take that pitch."

Consider this, hitter. The hitter who gears his stroke to hit the high strike can also take good cuts at the knee high pitch. But the hitter who gears his swing to the low strike seldom is able to take quality cuts at the high strike.

To hit the high strike effectively you will need: 1) a minimum of a 45-degree bat angle; 2) a "tall" stance; 3) plenty of top hand thrust; 4) keep the hands on top of the flight of the ball, and; 5) level shoulder rotation.

Ryne Sandberg rips a home run on a high pitch. Note the level hip and shoulder rotation, top arm extension, and angled front leg.

A tip on hitting the high strike from **Al Kaline**, one of the best high strike hitters of the game: "I don't think lead arm [weight shift] hitters are as effective in the upper part of the strike zone. The front arm tends to leave the bat further behind the ball. To hit the high pitch effectively, the top hand needs to be used."

Many hitting experts know that left-handed hitters tend to be better low ball hitters, but don't know why. (Conversely, left-handed hitters are poorer high ball hitters.) The reason is that most left-handed hitters are front side, lead arm, weight shift dominant. They can't get the bat into the upper part of the strike zone with authority! (Review Front Arm Verses Rear Arm in "Five Hitting Principles.")

Drills

A sequence to program your swing to the high strike. **Note:** Make sure you do not start out deeply crouched.

1. As you face the pitcher, take your prep, half-cuts in the high strike area. These preliminary cuts are for a *purpose*: you are programming your swing. Slice the high portion of the strike zone in half with the bat.

2. As you take these cuts, mentally tell yourself this is where you want the pitch. Say, "I want it *there*" and slice. "*I want it right there.*" Slice.

3. Gear your mechanics to operate in this zone. Keep the hands high. Start them on top of the ball's flight so you can come *down through* the plane of the pitch.

4. *Anticipate* the pitch in this zone.

If you program yourself this way you will find yourself *automatically* taking low pitches, because they are out of your frame of reference. If you find yourself unable to swing effectively in this high strike area you do not have level shoulder and hip rotation, your hands are too low in the launching position, or you have a vertical bat angle. You've got to level off on the high one.

GRIP

There is much debate involving the grip, often centering around the lining up of knuckles and such. Great hitters have held the bat all ways: 1) deep in their palms (Aaron) and; 2) higher up in their fingers (Musial, Dale Murphy). I preferred a light, relaxed grip at the base of the fingers 3) much like the one I used in pepper games. I always felt that tension before the swing slowed down my reactions a bit, sort of pinched off the quickness. But don't tell that to Aaron or Williams. They gripped firm and back in the hand. Ernie Banks, Dick Allen, and Rod Carew all gripped it lightly in the fingers. Use what is most comfortable and gives you the best results. Knowing a couple of principles will help you select what is best for you.

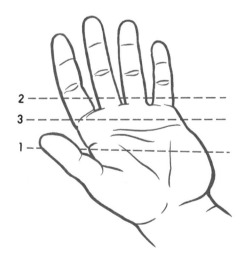

The thinner the handle and lighter the bat, the more it

tends to be held in the fingers because the fingers alone can't grip a thick bat well. Holding the bat more in the fingers may produce more whip, but it will cut down on the ability to shove, or push, with the meat of the hand. Consequently, finger-type grips are sometimes more effective with dominant front arm hitters.

Players who grip a thin handled bat in their fingers rely on the knob of the bat for stability. A hitter has little stability if he chokes up a thin handled bat. (Sal Bando was one of the few who choked up on thin handle bats.)

A thicker handled bat can be choked up with stability and held deeper in the palm for better shoving/pushing action. Because of this "shoving" action used to swing thick handled bats, which produces more contact, it has higher batting average potential for the hitter. This brings to mind the old bottle bats like Nellie Fox and Jackie Robinson used. Grips holding the bat deeper in the palm will allow the hitter to use a heavier bat. (Both Mantle and Maris used relatively thick handled bats.)

My advice: Experiment. Grip it firm, grip it light. Move the handle around in your hands. If you feel tense, lighten up, if you want more hand emphasis, firm it up. In the launch position you will start to firm up naturally, and as the swing starts both hands will be at maximum force. In his book, Ted Williams recommends an *extremely* firm grip. I believe he means the grip taken just prior to launching the bat. A firm grip puts the body's focus directly to the hands, where it should be.

Tip: Exert maximum hand strength from the launching position and you will be using your hands correctly.

Don Mattingly.

BALANCE AND RHYTHM

Question to **Frank Robinson:** What mechanical aspect comes to your mind first as the most important?

Robinson's answer: "Balance. With good balance your mechanics can take care of themselves."

Relaxed coordination of body parts *swinging at good pitches* produces balance, regardless of the style used. The soundest body mechanics in the world firing on pitches out of the strike zone will result in a loss of balance. If the hitter is swinging at good pitches and still experiences balance problems, they will most likely be due to over-swinging. The symptoms of over-swinging are: 1) extreme rotation; 2) uneven body segment rotation, including uppercutting; 3) tension, or; 4) pulling the bat through with the front side. For this hitter, it is back to the drawing board and tee.

Remember the words of **Richie Zisk:** "Hitting is a lot like dancing. A hitter needs rhythm and movement, not only with his bat but with his body as well. I'm a big believer in rhythm, hip rock, keeping the hitter in motion from the beginning."

Rhythm comes from repetitious, tension-free execution of proper mechanics. Remember that all hitting actions are done at a pace which allows all body parts to work together. These are "soft" movements. Nothing is done so fast that the body parts are rushed to keep up with each other. Big body actions involving the legs, hips, torso, and shoulders are done in a flowing, *fluid*, soft, swaying, relaxed manner. The hands come out of them with violent striking action. In every movement think relaxed, fluid, deliberate, good pitch, and you will get rhythm.

For the hands, think fast.

Frank Howard describes it this way: "First of all we've got to have some balance. We're on the balls of our feet. We've got a little rhythm going back and forth which is going to create weight shift. Weight shift back into a batting position to a weight shift forward with your swing, with the hips operating once you get to the hitting area. It comes together in a total swing."

Lesson 6:
Stroke Adjustments

Let's compare hitting to the construction of a house. Knowledge is the blueprint. Mechanical action is the foundation. *Adjustments* are the framework, siding, and roof. Adjustments allow the hitter to be successful by adapting to change. Mechanics are static, adjustments are dynamic. Every living thing which has ever been created—plants, animals, bacteria, solar systems, galaxies—are tested through the laws of adjustment. They either die out and make way for improvement, or survive through adjustment. The hitter is no different. I believe the major reason for my success over eighteen major league seasons was the ability to adjust many ways—the plane of my swing, the quickness of my hands, the movements in my pre-swing, my thinking, sometimes all within a single at-bat. You'll need this, too. The ability to adjust comes from practicing new and different ideas. The last thing you want to do is freeze yourself into a single way of thinking or swinging the bat.

STRIKE ZONE COVERAGE

Strike zone coverage is directly related to the hitter's size, position in the box, and his stride. The arms should be able to cover the outside half when they extend outward. Younger hitters will need to be closer to the plate, older and taller hitters can back off. The hitter can cover the whole strike zone if he is using his hands and extends his arms and bat *into* the strike zone from the side, rather than extending from back to front. With this physical concept, the batter extends his hands over the plate when swinging at an outside pitch, and pushes them forward on an inside pitch. This means he pushes the bat from inside the flight of the ball into the flight of the ball.

Harry Walker: "Good hitters' hands will go out if the ball is away, or they'll bring them in if it is on the inner half . . . it is important to try to learn to do this."

Pushing out on the outside pitch.   *Pulling in arms to tighten the swing on the inside pitch.*

These adjustments are the essence of the "swing-press" element, with hands leading the way. Ideally, extending forward to the inside pitch is done with the top hand and hip rotation. Extending outward to the outside pitch requires more front arm emphasis and weight shift. The hitter can make both adjustments when he gears his mechanics to the middle of the strike zone (Lau recommends the outside half) and adjusts this approach if the pitch is inside.

Ben Hines says the same thing with different words: "If the ball is on the outside part of the plate the arms move further away from the body. They reach a bit. As the ball gets closer to the inside part of the plate, the elbows get closer to the body." To get this action **Hines** adds, "Keep the barrel head back and extend the elbows and hands inside the ball's flight. You'll get plate coverage."

Drills

1. From your stance, press half cuts into all areas of the strike zone—in, out, up, down, the corners—from the side. Regard the strike zone as a large "6" domino chip with six white dots. Push the barrel of the bat at the different dots. Remember, you are not pushing just your hands at the different areas, you are pushing *the barrel of the bat*, led by the hands.

2. Much tee work on pushing the bat at different locations. Again, do not worry if the ball is not zinging off the tee—the pitcher's velocity colliding with the mass of the bat will provide the power. **Tip:** Hit the ball a couple of inches over the front edge of the plate on inside pitches, over the break of the plate for outside pitches.

Tip from Ben Hines: "As much as I can, I have my hitters look [gear their swings for] right down the middle. From there he can make his eight-to-ten-inch adjustment. It is virtually impossible to make a seventeen-inch swing adjustment from black to black."

FULL CUTS

Have you ever noticed how some hitters get your blood pumping as soon as they come to the plate, while others make you want to check the concession stand? Comparing them, the exciting ones are hitters who take quality, 100% cuts, at least up to two strikes. Their swings dominate the pitch. The boring hitters? They "feel" for the ball with maybe a 60% or 70% cut. The pitch dominates them. I won't bother to ask which are the good hitters.

When the count is in your favor, and you can afford to look for a certain pitch, or maybe you just *know* what pitch is coming, this is the time to execute your batting skill to the fullest by taking that full, clean, offensive cut. These are usually fast ball situations, although you can look for and time your full cut to the breaking pitch as well. Some keys to taking the quality cut:

1. As you take your half cuts at the pitcher, slice the zone where you want the pitch, programming your mechanics. As you do this you might be talking to yourself like this: "I'm looking for the

ball *right there.*" Slice. "It's gonna be right . . . there." Slice. "When it's right there I'm gonna drive it in the gap with backspin." Slice.

2. Anticipate the pitch in that zone. Expect it. Start your mechanics at this zone.

TWO STRIKE HITTING— THE PURE INSIDE-OUT STROKE

Hitting with two strikes calls for its own strategy. The hitter is in a hole, and he's forced to cover not just the entire strike zone, but every pitch in the pitcher's bag. He's forced to set his timing back but still have a hair-trigger. He has to maintain his aggressiveness, or even acquire more, since he has less time to work with.

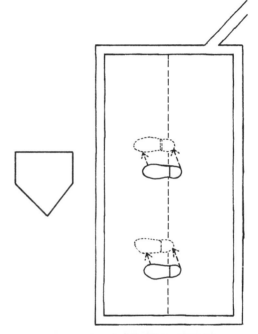

He can make a few physical adjustments. *First,* he can move a couple inches up and in toward the plate. This will put him closer to the breaking ball on the outside corner. *Second,* he can shorten up an inch or so on the bat, because he's forced to be quicker. *Third,* he can employ his inside-out stroke when tied up with inside fast balls while guarding the outside corner.

The hitter can also program his thinking. If he is facing the like-hander, he should be gearing his cut to the high, outside half of the strike zone. This will assure plate coverage and keep him from chasing the low breaking ball. Next, he can set his timing between the fast ball and curve ball and adjust his timing up or down with his hand speed.

Richie Zisk: "0-2, 1-2, I came off the bottom of the bat a little bit, and I moved a little closer to the plate. I pictured myself as a hockey goalie. Instead of keeping it out of the goal, I kept it out of the catcher's mitt. I would expect every pitch to be a strike until I couldn't swing at it."

Gearing the swing during preliminary cuts for the outside half with two strikes.

109

Glenn Wilson and I used to have pet sayings for this. One of us would say, "You gotta get down in there with it," and the other one would say back, "Yeah, you gotta stick your nose in it." It meant we had to get a little closer with two strikes, look over the outside corner, keep our head down and hit through the ball. Good two strike hitting is putting the ball in play, fighting off inside fast balls, and fouling off the pitcher's best pitch, anything to keep strike three out of the catcher's mitt.

Drill

1. Practice getting jammed off the tee. It's going to happen in a game, so you might as well practice it. Put the tee over the middle of the plate, inside corner. Practice hitting this ball over the first baseman's head. This will guarantee an extreme inside-out stroke. **Tip:** Use pure weight shift and avoid rotating the hips.

Keep the head down through contact.

KEEP YOUR HEAD DOWN

I think the key to the Hriniak/Boggs style is keeping the head down on contact. Much like the golf swing, the head stays down, eyes focused on the contact point until the ball is in flight. The longer the head stays "in the contact" the better vision you'll have. As you know, Boggs rarely swings and misses, seldom strikes out, and uses the whole field. This is an integral part of consistent contact. However, you should know that committing totally to "head down" will put a limit on home run production by dampening the hitter's power hitting. The power loss is caused because the unorthodox action of holding the head down in the contact area for an extra split second inhibits the body's natural turn through the ball.

My suggestion on "head down" is to try to get a feel for the mechanics of the action in batting practice. Whenever you get two strikes, employ this movement. Glue your eyes to the bat-ball contact. If it pays off, and it will, think about using it all the time.

HITTING TO THE OPPOSITE FIELD

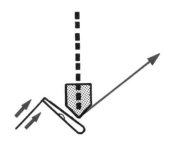

To be a complete hitter, you must be "in touch" with the opposite field. You have to own the ability to hit there. The key to hitting to the opposite field is allowing the ball to get over the plate before you make contact. As **Zisk** says, let it get deeper into your zone. You can't hit the ball out in front of the plate and get it to the opposite field. You almost have to think "let it get past me and I'll hit it out of the catcher's mitt."

Let me emphasize one thing which was a major key to my success. *You must be swinging down on the ball in order to let it get that far in on you.* If you're coming down from launch position to strike zone, you're leading with the hands which gives your bat the angle it needs to direct the ball the opposite way. Your swing will be very level, which will feel like down.

If you have any kind of "loop" in your swing you will have little or no success hitting to the opposite field. The hitter with the "loop," or uppercut, cannot let the ball get over the plate. He will foul it off or miss it, or at best fly out to the opposite field because his bat is under the ball. Hitting to the opposite field with an uppercut is next to impossible.

Richie Zisk has a good tip: "Try to hit the inside half of the ball. This makes you wait for the ball to come to you and forces the hitter to use the proper bat angle."

Opposite field hitting requires pure weight shift characteristics with hands leading the way.

Drill

1. Place the ball on the batting tee with the seams vertical, pointing backwards. Hit the inside seam. You will be demonstrating the push element of the swing necessary to opposite field hitting. Feel it.

FEAR AND TENSION

Charlie Lau said it best. "Nothing will stop a hitter as quickly as fear and tension at the plate." Yet as powerful as these devils are in spoiling a hitter, both fear and tension die to the act of usage. They fade away in time, if you work on them. If these two bullies are a problem for you, give yourself a fighting chance to rid yourself of them. Here is some help.

Fear

Don't be ashamed if you are afraid of being hit by the ball. There is fear connected with being so close to something flying by over which you have no control. I mean, who in his right mind would stand a couple of feet off an expressway with cars flying by if he didn't have to? So fear must be overcome. How? Experience through playing, getting hit, and getting out of the way enough times is the only way to learn.

There is always a bit of fear in the launch position against the like-hander, when you're looking for what pitch is coming. It's part of hitting. Hold your ground in the launch position with your hands back. *Hold your ground.*

In the launch position, the hips are still uncommitted with the front foot planted. With the front leg planted this way, it has the option of pushing the front hip back and around, or inward and closed. The leg should not push the hips open until the decision to swing (or start the hands) has been made. So if the pitch is inside, or head high, the front leg can push the body *closed* to roll it out of the way.

Drills

1. Have a teammate or coach toss tennis balls inside, and in the shoulder/head area, from a short distance. Practice rolling backward away until it becomes instinctive.

2. From behind a screen, have the teammate or coach toss strikes alternated with inside pitches, first one then the other, with tennis balls. **Key:** Keep your weight back until your hands start working.

3. Have the teammate or coach mix up the tennis ball pitches.

This is a good drill. It will teach you to keep your weight back and make the hands start the stroke.

Rod Carew suggests having a friend plunk you a few times with rubber baseballs or tennis balls to break down fear and realize it isn't that big a deal. This is sound advice.

Tension

Three keys can deflate your tension.

1. Take deep breaths just like a basketball player before a free throw. Oxygen is the body's natural tranquilizer.

2. Relaxed, tension-free arms and legs allow the nerve impulses to flow. Muscle tension "pinches" nerve impulses, and also causes tense muscles to "fight each other" rather than work together. Keep your body loose with stretching and "squeezing"—flexing followed by limp relaxation. In the wisdom of Satchel Paige, "Jangle around loosely as you move to keep the juices flowing."

   Do not be hyperactive.

3. The heck with anybody in the stands or either dugout. They don't count, only you and the pitcher do. Do not take counsel of outside influences.

One last word. Tension comes from the fear of failure. One thing you must learn to cope with in baseball is failure. You'll fail more than you'll succeed. Here's something that took me many years to learn: you must focus on your execution and not on the results. You've got no control of the results, only the execution. If you've practiced and practiced you should be confident in your execution, which should ease away tension. Also, don't try to do too much, just hit the ball with the "down" swing and everything will take care of itself.

Work these three helpers into your style. If fear and tension are your bullies, fight them and they will flee.

Lesson 7:
Mental Mechanics

Ted Williams said, "Hey, there's more to hitting than just walking up to the plate with the bat. You don't have to leave it all to chance. There are ways to prepare yourself by figuring out what the pitcher's going to throw."

The baseball graveyard is full of physically gifted players who mastered perfect mechanics for hitting batting practice, the Hall of Fame is not. The Hall of Fame is full of players who mastered the *skills of survival*, or, mental mechanics. They mastered four skills of survival—adjustment, adaptation, observation, and the application of strategy. Aside from their physical talent, these skills are the secrets of Hall of Fame success. If knowledge is the blueprint to building a house, and mechanics are the foundation, and adjustment the framing, siding and roof, then mental skills are the paint, shingles, shutters, and glass. They make the house salable.

Men, at least in society, compete with their minds. **Ted Williams** has gone on record as saying that 90 percent of hitting is mental. The better idea, the better plan, wins the day. The hitter has got to be smart. He may be able to outwit the pitcher, but the pitcher is teamed up with another hitter—the catcher—to defeat you. If that isn't enough, often a manager and a pitching coach with loads of experience are ready to aid them. You can bet they're planning strategy against you. And there you stand, all alone. You'd better be able to match wits with them.

I like the way **Clarence Jones**, Atlanta Braves hitting instructor, says it. "If you go up there without an idea, you're not hitting, you're just hacking."

Let's use the boxer as an example. Say that you have a boxer who is trained to throw perfect mechanical punches into the punching bag. Will this guarantee his success in the ring—that he will become a champion? Of course it won't. When he enters the ring many factors come into play which render punching mechanics secondary—defense, ring craftsmanship, anticipation, a fight plan, strategy, countering surprises, avoiding

114

strengths, capitalizing on weaknesses, condition, heart, the will to win. These have little to do with the punching bag. When the bell rings, he will be sorely tested on all of these skills.

The hitter is no different. He must analyze his opponent, the pitcher. The pitcher is programmed to upset his timing and exploit his weaknesses. For my money, I'll take the mechanical mess who has the skills of survival over the mechanically sound hitter who's sole skill is hitting the ball correctly off a tee.

The following skills will arm the hitter with a good grasp of what he needs to gain the mental edge. They are easy skills, but the discipline to use them will require effort.

KNOW YOUR OPPONENT

1. *What is the pitcher's strength?*

Each pitcher will have one skill that dominates his style, be it arm strength, control, breaking stuff, or finesse. The hitter's job is to figure out what his opponent's dominant skill is. From this comes a familiarity with the pitcher, which should eliminate surprise from his overall attack.

2. *What is the action of the pitcher's fast ball?*

No two fast balls are alike. Some rise, some sink. Some are cut like a small slider. And they vary in speed. Some are sneaky fast, others are broadcast as cannonballs by the pitcher's wind up. Some have heat, some rely on movement. Some are aspirin tablets, others beach balls. They come from different angles, with different movement and velocity.

This is the vocabulary which experienced hitters use to describe a pitcher's fast ball. Get your own terminology to distinguish different fast balls. Your first clues will come from the bench. Once you see them from the batter's box, commit them to memory. Become an expert on each pitcher's fast ball action.

Harry Walker: "You study every pitcher to see what his ball does. Maybe it moves away from you, maybe it moves in. And you remember it and adjust for it."

Richie Zisk: "I wanted to know, number one, the movement of the fast ball, whether it sunk, rose, which way it tailed. I needed to know. I wanted to know his fast ball so I could take it away from him."

Nice. So did I, Richie.

3. *What is the action of the pitcher's breaking ball?*

If your opponent has different breaking pitches, one of them will dominate. Is it a twelve-inch curve, or a four-inch slider, or maybe an eight-inch slurve? And how much slower than the fast ball is the breaking ball? Does it have loose spin or tight spin? A sharp break or a dull break? What's the angle of the break, vertical? Forty-five-degrees? A flat break? What is the angle of release? Get your clues from the bench. After you see the breaking ball first hand, commit it to memory.

4. *Does the pitcher have control of his breaking pitches?*

If you've been watching him, he'll let you know as soon as the second inning. The first inning he'll establish a pattern of breaking ball control. His second inning warm-ups will give you more clues; often you'll catch him working on the breaking ball when he is unsure of it. His second inning breaking pitches will either reinforce the first inning pattern or the jury is still out. By the third inning a pattern will be established. Use the 50 percent rule—if he is throwing less than 50 percent of his breaking pitches for strikes, he won't be able to throw it when he is behind in the count.

Frank Robinson: "They'd [other players] talk about how good a breaking ball somebody's got. What I want to know is, can he get it over the plate a majority of the time? If he can't, I'm going to eliminate it and hit off the other pitches, and that means the fast ball."

I'll take Frank's advice a step further. A pretty good rule of thumb for amateur hitters is not to swing at a breaking ball until you are forced to with two strikes. This will generally hold true for the professional hitter also, with a few exceptions. Take Nolan Ryan and Dwight Gooden, two premier right-handers of modern baseball. Not because they throw hard but because they both have "nose to toes" curve balls that are close to unhittable. I faced both Gooden and Ryan over a hundred times and I'd be lying if I told you I swung at five curve balls before I had two strikes. Why should I? I couldn't hit it hard or do much with it, so why swing at it? That's right, me, Mike Schmidt, couldn't do much with Gooden's curve ball. I could if I looked for it, but then I wouldn't do anything with his fast ball. Do you get it? So if it wasn't a 95 mph fast ball in my zone I took it and held out for one. The bigger and harder the break of the curve, the less it will be thrown for strikes. Two nasty Gooden curves in a row will get you a 1-1 or 2-0 count every time, and you can bet your house on a fast ball the third pitch. This is what mental hitting is all about. Take it from me, it's the only way to hit these guys.

The Percentage Pitch

With the tremendous velocity and curves that a big league pitcher can throw, do you think for one minute that a batter can consider each pitch in his arsenal and hit them all effectively? Not on your life. The professional hitter thinks in terms of the *percentage pitch* in a given situation.

The percentage pitch can be defined as one which can be predicted through previous observation and acknowledged pitchers' tendencies. It is the pitch which will come up a majority of times in a given situation, that is, six, seven, eight times out of ten. This is not to say that the hitter can't take a good rip at something else. He may, but by timing his mechanics to the most likely choice, he is putting himself in an optimum frame of mind to hit the percentage pitch with authority.

Frank Robinson: "I'm watching the pitcher to find out things—what he gets over consistently, what he likes to start a hitter off with, what he likes to throw when he's ahead or behind in the count, what he likes to finish a hitter off with, what he goes to in tough situations."

5. *Know the fast ball counts.*

Here they are— 1-0, 2-0, 2-1, 3-0, and 3-1. That's 42 percent of the possible ball-strike counts. You can afford to go on the offensive in these situations, looking for the fast ball where you want it and taking that quality, 100 percent cut. If the pitcher does not show you control of his breaking pitches, 0-0 and 3-2 counts become fast ball counts. That's 62 percent of the possible ball-strike counts in which the fast ball becomes the percentage pitch.

> **Fast Ball Counts:**
>
> 1-0, 2-0, 2-1, 3-0, 3-1, 0-0* and 3-2*

Richie Zisk: "Any time I was ahead in the count I became the aggressor. I thought in terms of driving the ball, maybe getting the barrel out in front."

Billy Williams: "It counts when you're ahead, you want to be a little more aggressive, not aggressive to pull the ball down the line because what you'll pull will be your front side off the ball. You want to be aggressive to right center and left center field. You're aggressive but you stay with the ball."

6. *Know the "neutral" counts.*

These are counts when you could get any pitch. The neutral counts are 1-1, and 2-2. Take a longer look at the ball in these situations. Don't try to pull the ball in these counts. And if the pitcher *has* control of his breaking pitches, 0-0 and 3-2 counts become neutral counts.

> **"Neutral" Counts:**
>
> 1-1, 2-2, 0-0*, and 3-2*

Breaking Ball Counts:
0-2, 1-2 and 3-2*

7. *Know the breaking ball counts.*

Here they are—0-2, 1-2, and 3-2 with a man in scoring position and first base open. In these counts the breaking ball becomes the percentage pitch, so you might as well guard against it. Adjusting to the fast ball can be accomplished by employing the inside-out stroke.

Naturally, there are more than these guidelines. When you bring in personalities, pennant races, coaching philosophies, weather, etc., the factors which determine a certain pitch approach infinity. And this is how it should be, leaving room for the smarter player. But these guidelines make a great rule of thumb to help you determine the percentage pitch.

GUESSING

Al Kaline: "Ted Williams always said, 'You're not really guessing. You're *looking for* a pitch.'"

Ted knew that guessing was absolute; you are either right or wrong. "Looking for" is more open, it factors in all the variables like movement, location, velocity, control, and timing. Also, "looking for" implies a take-it-or-leave-it attitude rather than right or wrong, and this develops the hitter's patience.

Always remember this: the smart hitter always knows the percentage pitch in a given situation. Then he gears his thinking to the speed, movement, and location of that percentage pitch. If he has anticipated incorrectly, he uses his hands to make up the difference or takes the pitch. Hitting is timing your stroke to the pitch. Smart hitting is the delicate process of adjusting this timing to the percentage pitch.

Richie Zisk gives an example of this: "If I'm coming up in the bottom of the ninth where one swing of the bat ends it, chances are the pitcher is not going to let himself get beat with a fast ball, so I have to look out over the plate. I've already eliminated one pitch and half the plate, until I'm ahead in the count."

These mental mechanics are what the old-timers used to talk about on the train rides from city to city. They allow the heady player to separate himself from the crowd. To acquire these skills, all the hitter needs is some memorization, common sense, a willingness to learn, and of course, practice. Unlike re-programming physical movement, which may be right or wrong and require time, these skills can help overnight. And no one will argue their benefits.

If you are in professional baseball and are not in tune with this hitting philosophy, you are missing the boat. If you are an amateur, work hard at these ideas as best you can and you'll get your chance as a pro. I know you'll know what pitch is coming 75 percent of the time. I did.

OBSERVATIONAL SKILLS

Application of the previous seven rules depends on your agreement with the following points: **1)** the hitter is more successful when he knows what pitch is coming; **2)** the hitter is more successful when he knows the movement and velocity of that pitch, and; **3)** the hitter is more successful when he knows a given pitcher's tendencies in a given situation. If you agree with these points, here is the application.

Bullpen Observation

The serious hitter takes the time to observe a good sampling of the pitcher's bullpen warm-ups. From the dugout, the pitcher will appear small, like in the view finder of a camera. In time, the hitter's eye will be trained to get an accurate bearing of the pitcher's motion, angle of release, ball movement, velocity, and control. And usually, the angle from the dugout is ideal for reading pitch movement.

Many times you will catch the pitcher with his pitching coach working on something that isn't quite right. When you do, see if the problem continues in the game. Remember, whatever enters the pitcher's mind will eventually come out of his arm.

Warm-Up Observation

The pitcher's eight warm-ups before the game and between innings move you closer to what you have observed in the bullpen. Take note of his hand signals to the catcher. He'll be signalling movement on every pitch he's got with his glove. He'll also be showing you the location of his release point. When he releases the pitch, track it all the way to the catcher to gauge speed and action.

Frank Robinson: "I didn't need information as to how hard a guy was throwing, or how big a breaking ball he had. I could see that for myself."

You'll get an even better perspective when standing in the on-deck circle, or next to home plate if you are leading off the inning or they are making a pitching change. Hurry into these positions when they are available.

Observing the First Hitters

Closely observe the action of the hitters ahead of you. Note their timing and what might be surprising them. If they get fooled by a pitch it might fool you, too. This will give you additional confirmation of what you have observed in the bullpen, and in the pitcher's warm-ups. When the first hitters return to the bench, don't miss the opportunity to ask them what they have seen. Your timing will start out similar to theirs. They have first-hand information you need.

Pitchers do not have nine different game plans, one for each hitter. Generally, they'll try to get you the same way they got the guy ahead of you, unless the game situation changes. Trade information throughout the game with your teammates. I used to do this with Pete Rose a lot. He knew everything. He'd tell me how a pitcher used to pitch Bench or Perez, and then the guy would try it on me. I'd be waiting for him. Pete could tell if the guy had his good slider, and if he didn't, what he'd go to in place of it. He could tell you when the guy was changing his pitching pattern, so you didn't need to make an out before you could adjust. I'd help him too, but he really didn't need it. He was generally a step ahead of the good observer. He helped me a lot more.

The more you observe about the pitcher, the more clues you will get to defeat him. Some hitters watch every delivery, like Rose. They see pitching patterns, pitching strategy, strategy breakdowns, changes in motion and velocity. The more you know about your opponent, the better prepared you are to win.

Ted Williams: "It's really not so complicated. It's a matter of being observant, of learning through trial and error, of picking up things. You watch a pitcher's warm-ups. If he isn't getting the breaking ball over you can think about waiting for the fast ball. Now you can sit on the bench, pick your nose, scratch your back side, and you're the loser. The observant guy will get the edge. He'll take the advantage of every opening. For me guessing was observing . . . knowing what you're swinging at, knowing the pitch you hit or missed. Knowing the pitcher's pattern."

Ted Williams was *one* of the game's greatest hitters. Ted Williams was *the* game's greatest thinker. Without his hitting strategy he'd have been just another good hitter.

A...B...C...

Lesson 8:
Hitting Simplification Strategies

PITCH INFORMATION

The first pitch of the day is very valuable. In most cases this pitch should be taken for at least five reasons: 1) you can gain much information about the pitcher and his approach by what he throws on the first pitch; 2) you can practice your own rhythm and balance against his delivery; 3) you'll prevent a quick at-bat so the hitter behind you can get information; 4) you may have ball-one thrown, or a nasty borderline pitch, and you have a definite fast ball count on the second pitch; 5) TO LOCATE THE PITCHER'S RELEASE POINT. All of these are good reasons for taking the first pitch. However, if there is a tough customer on the mound and a man in scoring position, I've been known to look fast ball and smoke it on the first pitch.

This follows Ted Williams' theory of "don't swing at anything you haven't seen first." If the same pitch comes up again, you'll time its action. And if not, you accrue more knowledge that will come in handy on later trips. This strategy applies only to the first at-bat of the game. If you are pinch-hitting, or see a new pitcher later in the game, you've got to strike at the first good pitch you see. You can't afford to take a strike in these later situations.

HARD THROWERS AND LEFTY-LEFTY SITUATIONS

When you're facing a hard thrower, or find yourself up against a pitcher who is tough on you, as in lefty-lefty situations, look only for the fast ball up until two strikes. Remember, the fast ball is the easiest pitch to throw for strikes, particularly for a left-hander. And eliminating the curve makes hitting much easier. Often, when the hitter faces a tough "like-hander" he has a tendency to "bail out," or, pull off the ball by opening up the front side to the pitcher's motion rather than to the ball. Knowing this, he must discipline himself to stay in, keep the front side closed, keep his head on the pitch, and use his hands.

121

I had a saying that applied to this teaching. "Every at-bat will contain at least one fast ball to hit. Your job is to find it." Get your plan together.

Everything is a part of the whole in hitting. Before the at-bat you have catalogued a degree of information to do battle with. During the at-bat, if your plan is good, you will be able to work yourself into favorable counts. Hitting in favorable counts, the fast ball counts, where you can swing down on that level plane, will make you a tremendous hitter at any level. Remember, the opposition can't consistently defend against hard hit ground balls, but they can catch every fly ball.

Billy Williams, Hall of Fame left-handed hitter, on facing left-handed pitchers he was not familiar with: "There would be some left-handed hitters in our lineup. I'd look at how this guy pitched to our guys. In my mind I'd have some kind of plan from this. And I'd watch the velocity of the fast ball, how his curve ball breaks, how many of each pitch he threw. So when I left the on-deck circle I had a plan on what to expect, what to sit on."

Does a hitter ever want to look curve ball? **Frank Howard:** "That's where knowing your pitcher comes in, which comes from watching him. If a guy is getting his breaking ball over and he's giving it to everybody, you can lay on it for a strike or two. But if there's any doubt, hit off the fast ball."

SELF-TALK

The on-deck circle is the place for observation.

Without a positive frame of mind, a hitter cannot excel. Let's talk about building instant confidence.

Self-talk is a way of vaccinating yourself against fear, tension, and low confidence. Is that little voice inside of you talking positively? Is it building you up or tearing you down? If it is negative, you are programming yourself to fail. You've got many opportunities to prime yourself with positive self-talk all over the field. Let's concentrate on two places—the on-deck circle and in the batter's box.

The on-deck circle is the place for observation. As the hitter is picking up information, he can also build himself up. While he is watching, he might be talking to himself like this:

"I can hit this guy. I've hit better pitchers than this before. He's no better than I am. If he throws me that same pitch I'm gonna kill it. I'm takin' full cuts, and when I connect he's gonna pay. I'll look for his fast ball and when it comes in I'm gonna blast it. I'm the guy with the skill, I'm the guy who's gonna win. I'm studied and prepared. Today is my day. I know I'm gonna get a base hit."

Believe me, it works. What have you got to lose? What you'll get is a lift in confidence when you step in.

The hitter can do the same thing when he gets to the batter's box. He analyzes his situation, gets his plan, then self-talks himself into a positive frame of mind.

CONFIDENCE

Ask yourself, what is the main difference between a hitter in a slump and a hitter on fire? It's that wonderful yet elusive feeling of confidence, confidence, confidence. Maybe you saw the movie "City Slickers" where Billy Crystal tells his buddy what the secret of life is. He holds up his index finger and says, "It's just one thing." Sometimes that's all it takes. You've got to find what that one thing is for you.

Confidence as a hitter is found and kept in different ways by every hitter. It wasn't until my thirteenth year, 1985, that I found my way of staying confident every day, and it can work for you. Here's what happened to me.

I was facing Doc Gooden in July of 1985. I'd been struggling since opening day. I couldn't find a consistent anything. It didn't help that I started the season one for twenty-six. Anyway here I am with a man on third and one out against the best pitcher in the league. I knew from batting practice about swinging "down" on the ball. I'd seen Dick Allen do it over the years but never really could convince myself to do it in a live game. In that at-bat, for some reason, I said, "What the heck, I'm gonna swing down on any pitch he throws me. Just like Dick Allen used to do."

I fouled off a curve ball. Then he threw me his best fast ball and I tomahawked it, really chopped down. The noise was like a gun shot but the feel was weightless. When I looked up the ball was on its way toward the right-center field scoreboard, about 450 feet away. Rounding second base, I vowed to swing down through the ball every swing for the rest of my career. From that at-bat through 1988 until I hurt my shoulder I hit over .300. Me, a former strikeout artist, averaging over .300 for over two full seasons. My strikeouts went from 120 a year to less than 90. I wasn't fouling off pitches with an uppercut anymore. I won my third MVP at the age of 36 in 1986, and I had a similar year in 1987.

Confidence for me came from a belief in that single fundamental. It was my "one thing." I began realizing that I would hit the ball hard more often by swinging down, which was actually very level. Any pitch, any location, day or night.

You must find for yourself what that "one thing" is for you. It could come from self-talk, a chance occurrence, or an experiment such as I had. Keep your ears and eyes open at all times.

Lesson 9:
Advanced Hitting Strategies

CREATING ROOM: Tightening up the Swing

The like-handed hitter has less time to work. From his line of vision, he must wait a split second longer to judge the pitch and still be able to protect himself on inside fast balls. He must be faster against the like-hander. He learns to do this two ways, which tighten and quicken his swing.

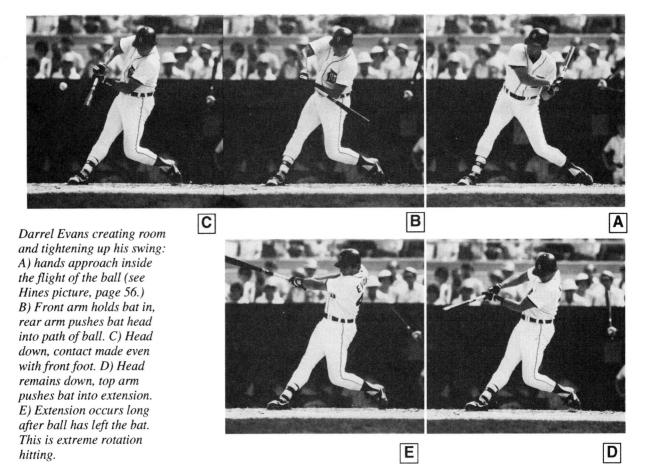

Darrel Evans creating room and tightening up his swing: A) hands approach inside the flight of the ball (see Hines picture, page 56.) B) Front arm holds bat in, rear arm pushes bat head into path of ball. C) Head down, contact made even with front foot. D) Head remains down, top arm pushes bat into extension. E) Extension occurs long after ball has left the bat. This is extreme rotation hitting.

1) The hitter stops his forward weight shift by offering resistance with an angled, firm front leg, stopping his forward movement. Now his front leg repels the weight shift and pushes the hips around into rotation. Rotating the hips (the shot-putter) takes less space than shifting the weight forward (the javelin thrower).

2) The hitter can tighten the arc of his swing with pronounced top hand action and by allowing *neither* arm to gain full extension. The hitter brings his hands, wrists, and elbows closer to his body. With this, the arc of the swing tightens and increases its velocity.

All power hitters employ these methods to "create more room" when quickness to pull the ball are needed. Frank Robinson and Johnny Bench were great examples of this technique, as are José Canseco and Mark McGuire. Distance taken away from the weight shift creates more distance to hit the pitch. By tightening up the swing, bat speed can be increased because the tighter the arc of the stroke, *the faster the bat travels*. Also, by using the hands, wrists, and elbows, power is not decreased.

Hitter tightening up his swing by allowing neither arm to extend.

Drill

1. Tighten the arc of your swing with dry swings using only the hands, wrists, and elbows. Do not give yourself full extension of either arm. Use full hip rotation by pushing back on the hips with a heavily angled front leg.

This action may make you feel you are swinging like a sissy, but I wouldn't call Canseco or McGuire or Johnny Bench sissies. They hit a lot of home runs using it. Tight swings like these are analogous to the boxer using short punches in a clinch.

WARNING: The hitter must be careful *not* to eliminate his weight shift and allow his back leg to collapse. If this happens the hitter essentially "sits down" in pure rotation without a trace of weight shift. This will not work. Instead of this, the hitter should "compress" his weight shift with an unyielding front leg. Stay tall.

DEVELOPING YOUR EYE

Charlie Lau: "Take the pitches you can't swing at. Swing at the pitches you can." Charlie meant, if the hitter can't take a healthy swing at a given pitch because of timing problems or pitch location, it is good hitting not to swing. If his timing is right and the pitch is hittable, then it is good hitting to swing.

Words are sometimes poor describers, so take your time on this section.

Say that the hitter is facing a pitcher throwing 90 miles-per-hour. Thrown at this speed the pitch is more of a streak than a ball. The hitter has about four-tenths of a second to "load" his mechanics, see the pitch, and execute his swing.

The hitter sets up, anticipates a pitch over the plate, and gears his swing mechanics for a pitch over the center of the plate. Say the pitcher cuts loose with one that comes in two feet off the outside corner (ball #9 below). Does the hitter swing? No. Why not? Because his swing can't reach it! Also, the pitch is away from the center of the plate, which his swing is geared for. To reach the pitch two feet off the plate the hitter would have to contort his body so much and become so inefficient that it is not feasible to swing. *His body refuses the effort, not out of sophistication so much as uncoordinated work.*

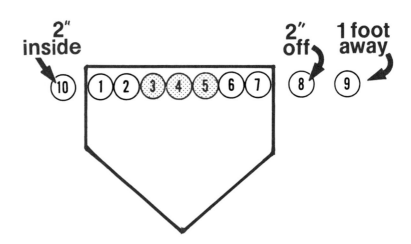

Let's say the hitter gears his swing to handle balls 3, 4, and 5. This means that his swing will be efficient and accurate on the three balls over the heart of the plate. His swing will be *less* efficient (and require more work) on balls 2 and 6, and even less efficient (requiring even more work) on balls 1 and 7, because the hitter will have to bend at the waist and adjust his swing away from optimum force.

To hit balls 8 and 10 would require massive bending at the waist, leaning back on the heels, drastically reaching or drawing in the arms—which would subtract efficiency and coordination. Or, in other words, to swing at a pitch two inches off the corner requires much deviation from the good, full, offensive cut. *The cut requires more work but becomes less efficient. It would result in only a 60 percent to 75 percent force. The hitter who feels his body begin these inefficient movements as they are happening can shut them down and take the pitch.*

This is how great hitters like Ted Williams and Al Kaline could take pitches off the corners of the plate without flinching. Because their whole approach was geared for a pitch in an area, and it didn't come up, they didn't move their bat. The pitch location wouldn't allow good cuts. Their muscles refused the effort. With practice and concentration, you can *feel* when a certain pitch is uncomfortable to hit.

Drills

1. Practice efficient, offensive dry cuts. Next . . .

2. Practice dry, 60 percent to 75 percent cuts at imaginary pitches that are off the corners, high and low, out of the strike zone.

In time you will feel the difference in body movement between good and bad cuts. Your mind will develop rapport with your muscles. You'll have a good eye.

Getting Your Pitch (Ultra-Advanced Hitting)

Ted Williams said it. "You've got to get a good ball to hit." I'm right there with him. Mainly because if you aren't selective of what you're swinging at, your at-bats are filled with poor, ineffective swings which produce weakly hit outs. Exceptional hitters are exceptional not because they necessarily have a knack for hitting the center of the ball, but because of the pitches they choose to swing at. Consequently, they swing with quality which produces hard hits. Let me say that again a different way because it is very important. Exceptional hitters choose good strikes to swing at; lesser batters are not as selective. Take two different batters with equal ability. One swings at whatever his bat will reach, regardless of timing or location. The other only swings when his timing is right, at pitches he can take good swings at, up to two strikes. The first batter hits .240 to .260. The second will hit .300-plus. The skill of "getting your pitch" is what refines major league hitters.

Let's say that you have studied and practiced, and you have developed a proficient, sophisticated eye at the plate. You have developed the ability to take the balls and swing at the strikes. And with this ability comes proficiency at running the count to your favor a majority of the time. You find yourself in more 1-0, 2-0, 2-1, 3-1, and 3-0 counts. In these counts, the finely tuned hitter not only has his choice of pitches, *he has his choice of strikes.* Or, he can further refine the strike zone into preferred zones. **Richie Zisk** and **Al Kaline** have good ways of explaining this.

Richie Zisk: "When the count is 1-0, 2-0, 3-1, 3-0, I'm in an offensive situation. If I'm looking for a particular pitch in these situations, usually a fast ball, and I don't get it, I'm not going to make an adjustment to hit this ball. I am going to let it go by. If I'm looking fast ball, and it's almost the one I want but not quite, I've still got to lay off.

"Say I'm looking for a fast ball in these counts out over the plate, something I can drive [balls 3, 4, and 5]. I would concede the inside corner, so I give the pitcher the first ball or two on the inside corner [of the diagram], and maybe one or-one-and-a-half balls on the outside corner. If I swung at these pitches, in these counts, it was a major hitting mistake. Major because I had the advantage but didn't hit my pitch.

"The same is true on timing. If the pitcher doesn't throw into my timing when I'm ahead, with less than two strikes, I take that pitch. I'm not going to make big adjustments in my timing. I'll take that pitch."

Al Kaline: "Try to be patient [take the borderline pitches] until the pitcher makes a mistake."

Realize that in these situations—1-0, 2-0, 2-1, 3-1, 3-0—you are not penalized by taking a pitch that fools you or is out of your timing. You are either still ahead or the count is evened.

Drills

1. Have a teammate toss tennis balls from a short distance so that he will be able to pinpoint his accuracy. He should call out the count and then throw pitches in and out of the zone. Example: He calls "Two balls and no strikes" and then throws either a ball in your zone or completely out of the strike zone. Practice hitting the balls in your zone and taking the rest.

2. Same drill except include curves and change-ups alternated with fast balls. To duplicate timing, the hitter should be using the same size bat he would in a game. Lay off the pitches out of your timing.

3. Good, full cuts will be your feedback. Anything less and you should have taken it.

Lesson 10:
Improvement Strategies

PSYCHOLOGICAL PLOYS

I once knew a sports psychologist who spent one hour with a college basketball forward. He had the player close his eyes and imagine himself as a leopard on the court. The player saw himself as a black leopard in a basketball uniform, prowling for rebounds, because that was this player's job. The player saw himself leaping way up above the rim to take errant shots off the glass, prowling on defense, beating his opponent into position with quick, graceful strides, crouching beneath the rim before leaping high into the air. He set a school record for rebounds his next game. His mind saw himself in different, faster, and more powerful terms to do his job.

If you have some idle time, envision yourself similarly, according to your job. Sit in a quiet room. Close your eyes. Take six slow, deep breaths. Take a minute or two to relax. Clear your mind. On the picture screen in your mind, create images. Maybe you're an ultra strong, hairy beast toeing dirt in the batter's box, saliva dripping out of your mouth, handling the bat like a toy, able to wait until the last instant before striking with superhuman strength. If so, watch him all the way from stepping into the box to driving the ball and racing to first base. Watch him through an entire at-bat, then become him.

Or maybe you're a lithe deer at the side of the plate, laying down a perfect drag bunt, bursting out of the box with instant racing speed, sprinting as though you've been flushed out into the open from the bushes, trying to outrun a hunter's bullet.

Maybe you see yourself locked in a sound chamber with only you and the pitcher inside. His pitches are the size of softballs, all thrown through a clear pipe into the heart of the strike zone. Maybe you imagine your bat emitting sparks of energy, your hands like an engine, and the noise of contact like a powerful gunshot.

STRENGTH PROGRAMS

Any overall conditioning program is beneficial to the body. A strength program which is comprehensive, devoting work to all the muscles, cannot do anything but help you. Ask yourself, would you be a better hitter if you were five percent stronger than you are now? Ten percent?

A Nautilus-type program, or a weight program which strengthens the entire body is best. Don't forget the legs. They are the foundation to every muscle movement you make as a hitter. Extra strength work need only be done on the hands and wrists. A good share of stretching should be done. Any time spent on the bench with a muscle pull costs you at-bats. Worse, it let's somebody else do your job. You see muscle pulls all the time in the major leagues. Spend a good ten minutes every day stretching your quads, hamstrings, and groin until you can do the splits. For the younger player, in all probability you are involved in another sport during the off-season. As soon as you are committed to baseball get into a program of hard work with weights and cardiovascular exercises at least three days a week. Find a group of guys with the same goals and work together. Never quit or procrastinate in your workout. See your goals and force yourself to attain them. Hard work is always rewarded.

BUNTING

Bunting is entirely mechanical and is covered adequately in a number of texts. Rod Carew's book, *Art and Science of Hitting* is suggested. Have bunting in your arsenal. The bottom line to bunting is this: If you *want* to be a good bunter, if you *will* it, you'll acquire the technique and practice until you are.

Every hitter who takes pride in his skill should be a good bunter. It has all the earmarks of professionalism. Look at it. Delicate, practiced touch, finesse, surprise, sacrifice, secrecy, cunning, trickery, strategy, few do it well. Steve Garvey was the best. If he caught you back at third, bingo! Over the years he must have gotten a dozen hits past me because I had to play a couple steps in on him. Multiply that by every team in the league, then add in the bunt hits, and that's how effective it is. I wish I'd done it more.

Even the best hitters are asked to sacrifice bunt. Here are some tips to become professional at it:

1. Move closer to the front of the box.

2. Grip the bat lightly to absorb the shock.

3. Hold the bat head slightly higher than the handle.

4. See the ball hit the bat.

5. Keep your head down until the bunt is on the ground.

6. Get serious about it.

BATTING PRACTICE

Al Kaline: "I think hitters today concentrate too much on hitting the ball out of the ballpark in batting practice. My concentration was on hitting the line drive, reacting with two strikes, reacting to where they were going to pitch me. Instead of trying to generate a lot of power, I was trying to fine tune."

Al's right. Pre-game is the time to get in the right frame of mind. Try for crisp line drives straight away, and get a feel for the opposite field. The worse thing you can do is try to hit a bunch of home runs.

Workout batting practice is the time to work on a particular problem. During this time remember: it's not how many swings you get but how much you concentrate on each swing. This is a chance to develop good habits through repetition. The best hitters take the most batting practice. If you could measure the number of batting practice cuts in a career you'd find these names in the top ten: Williams, Rose, Yastrzemski, Boggs, Schmidt, Gwynn, and Puckett.

SLUMPS

First, a hitter is always riding out waves of absolute confidence/less confidence, good mechanics/struggling mechanics, good thinking/bad thinking, good luck/bad luck. Heaven is when the good are working together. Problems occur when the negatives join hands.

Here is a typical slump syndrome: The pitcher gets the hitter out a few times too many. The hitter panics. One or more of the negatives gets into his head, making his *imagined* bad streak real. Bad thinking takes hold. Tension begins seeping into the muscles. More outs. An examination of imagined faulty mechanics comes into view. The hitter begins grabbing at remedies for his "slump," further making his problems reality. Lo, he finds some. He works like a dog and begins to feel deserving of a few hits. Finally, the law of averages gives him some. He regains confidence, relaxation. Finally, the law of averages begins swinging back his way. Meanwhile, his average has fallen fifty points.

A remedy? Always work on your hitting, in good times and bad. Always feel deserving. A mechanical flaw is not the reason for the vast majority of slumps. Hitters can hit well with flaws. Only when those flaws become reasons for a slump do they have their effect. Bad thinking is the problem more often. Give the pitcher some credit. The law of averages favors him, and sometimes he's going to get you out several times in a row. Just like sometimes you'll get three hits in one game. You can hit .450 for a stretch with a mechanical flaw just like you can hit .150 for a stretch with perfect mechanics. It is the law of averages at work.

Keep swinging. You'll have to swing to get out of it. Pay more attention to seeing the ball out of the pitcher's hand by controlling your head movement and tracking the ball into the strike zone with your head down. *Work at keeping your hits on the ground and out of the air.* Take it from a guy who was in some deep slumps. When you're in a slump, everything in the air is dead meat. It seemed like, until I got my confidence back, the only hits I ever got in a slump period were ground balls. Even my line drives seemed to get caught. Any time you're swinging and keeping the ball on the ground you've got a good chance at hits.

Tips: Work a little harder on defense during a dry period. It will give you the "deserving" feeling sooner, and will help your club regardless of your hitting. Also, keep up good teammate relations. Encourage and pull for them at all times. When you're going bad, you'll need their support.

Lesson 11:
The Best Drills

Scores of drills have been developed to burn in certain movements with repetition, and many of them are good. Some are ingenious. If the movement being worked is advantageous, much can be accomplished. Each coach has his "pet" drills, so it would be useless to prescribe favorites. But I'll stand behind six universals.

1. Pepper

No hitting drill can match the lessons obtained through this wonderfully simple game. It can be said that hitting is a big pepper game—just add a stride and a follow-through and you're hitting. Hip rotation cannot be exercised fully during pepper, but everything else can be worked on, learned, and *realized*, even the weight shift. First, you are forced to use your hands. Second, you will make contact over the plate. The push, the inside-out, stroke is utilized. Square contact is the goal. Crisp, line drive contact is paramount. Loose hands, some weight shift, all field use, rhythm, balance—they are all there. Level body action is a must. One coach remarked, "I can line up all my hitters in pepper games. The ones who hit good pepper are my good hitters. Those who don't will need a lot of work." He's right. Hit as much pepper as you can, and take note of what is happening.

The great hitters are all good pepper players. Pepper has become a lost art. See if you can bring it back.

2. "Dry" cuts

"Dry" cuts means swinging the bat without a ball. Whenever a ball is involved in a drill, either in throwing it to a hitter or having it rest on the tee, the hitter's attention is on the ball rather than the stroke. Leave the ball out of it and give your full attention to your swing—the movements, the "whoosh," your balance and rhythm. Focus your mind on ways to make it faster, more efficient, healthier, more forceful. And the beauty of dry cuts is that you can work on things without a field, equipment, or teammates if they aren't available. You have no time limit. You can work on things listening to a ball game over the radio or watching one on television. And each swing can be a perfect one. Actors memorize their parts in solitary confinement, and they turn in beautiful performances. So can the hitter. All you need is a bat.

Harry Walker: "Hitters don't spend enough time just swinging the bat."

Practice fifty cuts, 100 cuts, 500 cuts, 1,000. Just don't take all the medicine in one day

3. Tee work and short toss

Use these as a graduation from "dry" rehearsal. Remember, any time you bring a ball into the situation, attention begins leaving your body parts. Know that in tee work, the hitter supplies all the power. This is why he wants to place the tee way out in front of the plate—so he can unwind with a lot of rotation—something he can't do at home plate. Hit off the tee with good mechanics, not overrotation with a huge arc that produces a lot of noise. This same huge arc aimed at a pitch out in front of the plate will produce nothing but silence in the game. Power comes from square contact. The speed of the pitch colliding with the mass of your bat in square contact will give you all the power you need.

Toward the end of my career I used the tee almost everyday. So much can be practiced in such a small area, by yourself or with a teammate.

4. Watch major league games

With the proliferation of sports coverage on television, and an average of two big league games broadcast daily during the baseball season, many "secrets" contained within the game of baseball are broadcast with them, oftentimes from different camera angles, stop action, slow motion, and pointed out by an old pro.

It is getting to the point where every big league game is a clinic for coaches and players. Watch the hitters. Hip action, momentum devices, hand action, everything is available at the flick of a dial. Particularly watch the good hitters compared to the not so good. See if you can identify their mechanics. See if they are hitting with the count.

5. Time your pitcher's warm-ups in the bullpen

Much can be gained here in rhythm, balance, timing, momentum, release point, and pitch reading. It is also a great place to work on your pre-swing into the launch position. And usually the pitcher appreciates a hitter standing in.

6. Practice by swinging a heavier wooden bat

This will force your body into using rhythm, knee cock and a small hitch. The crime of light metal bats is that they can allow the hitter to hit with "dead" hands from a dead stop position. This won't teach rhythm and timing. Swinging a heavier wooden bat develops body momentum. It also strengthens the wrists, hands, and forearms.

Richie Zisk on the aluminum bat: "I think the aluminum bat is not allowing the hitter to learn proper mechanics—almost no hip rotation, no starting of the hands or cocking the bat. The bats are so light the hitter doesn't need these. I see a lot of 'wrapping' [tilting the bat behind the head as a starting point]. Then he gets a wooden bat in his hands and his mechanics are so poor that it's difficult to adjust to wood [if he signs a pro contract.] Old habits are very hard to break."

Lesson 12:
My Four Keys to Success

The points I have covered so far are what I learned in over thirty years of baseball, almost twenty as a major league player. They are the end product of countless hours of thinking and re-thinking, trial and error, watching miles of videotape, picking coaches' brains, and banging away at hundreds of thousands of pitched baseballs. This teaching is what I have come to know about the truth in hitting a baseball. Other experts may disagree here and there, but I know that if they have studied as extensively, they will agree with the overwhelming majority of what I have to say. Hopefully, this knowledge will serve as a series of shortcuts to you, something on which to build your foundation. If you are fortunate to study as extensively as I have, you will come to the same conclusions.

These, I believe, are the ultimate keys to any success.

1. Desire

No doubt, I was blessed with some physical gifts which allowed my career to turn out as well as it did. Believe me, I'm thankful. But my career could have just as easily floundered and died. I could have wasted my talent. In addition to my physical gifts, I had something almost spiritual working for me. I was blessed with a lion's share of, for lack of a better word, desire. Like my ability, this also was a gift. When I was at the crossroads of whether to progress or decline, and there were many of these, somehow I took the right road and progressed. I cannot say exactly why this happened. I can only describe it, and by describing it, perhaps it will allow you to take the right roads at the crossroads of your own career.

You might not believe me if I told you I couldn't really hit a curve ball until I was twenty-five years old, but it's true. That's why I tried switch hitting. My first year in pro ball I hit around .200. I learned to guess a little bit, which helped out, but my first year in the majors I struggled along at .190 for six months. The thought of quitting, or that I'd never learn how to hit, was always present. All I can say is, I wouldn't buy into it. Instead, I chose to believe that there was a way, and that I wouldn't quit until I found it. So, instead of giving up, I chose another purpose: keep going ahead until I found the answers. Sure enough, by not giving up, I found them and kept finding them all the way to that desperate home run I hit off Gooden in 1985.

In analyzing my long run of perseverance, I come up with four words to describe my development as a standout major league player. The first is *patience*. Not that I didn't want the answers yesterday, but when I didn't get them I was patient with myself. I didn't go beating myself up when I continued to struggle. I thought about things. If I was going to move myself from an average, sometimes awkward young player into a pro prospect, I knew it wouldn't happen over night. It would take season after season, if it was going to happen. So I concentrated on small steps, fitting one brick into place at a time and cementing it firmly. I started over from scratch again tomorrow when necessary, every tomorrow. A young player has time to work with, so you can afford some patience.

Faith. Faith is believing in something which cannot be seen, heard, or proved. It is believing in a thought, an idea. I had faith that hard work would someday pay off. I had no proof it would, I just believed it. To be honest, this was not always faith in myself, because there were times when I wondered. But faith that if I kept working, didn't give up, something good would happen. Eventually it always did. I'll tell you how important faith is. The word confidence, what you will need on the field and in life, comes from two Latin words—*con* meaning with, and *fideo* meaning faith. "With faith" is confidence. Without faith is zero confidence. That's how important faith is.

I had *dedication.* I wanted to be the best ballplayer I could be, and I was dedicated to that purpose. That was what I wanted to be, and I let nothing humanly possible get in the way of that goal. Again, lots of things tried to stop me—ill-intentioned people, drugs, tough, older pitchers, night life, failure, the curve ball—but I took a tough stand against them. In other words, you say something like this to yourself: "I will never stop working to get better, no matter how unsuccessful I may be. I will persevere despite the failure I know will come." And then you do.

Confidence. This was the toughest one to get and keep, because it is so illusive to everyone. Just when you think you've got a firm grip on it, it threatens to leave. I find this: if you make yourself have the other three—patience, faith, and dedication, confidence will come to roost with them. Why? Because it is made from them.

It boils down to a mind game. You choose to get these qualities into your life, and you let nothing get in their way. That anyone can do. Be faithful long enough, you'll have them. I say this in the same spirit of giving you knowledge of hitting skills. *This is what worked for me.* The only explanations I have for persevering was that I wanted to, I chose to, and I did.

2. The level cut/ground ball/line drive theory

When I finally learned hitting well enough to get my career moving steadily ahead, a couple of questions really played on me. Why are 90 percent of all swings uppercuts? Why is there such an affinity for hitting the ball in the air, when the vast majority sock your average and hurt your team? Ever since we were little kids playing in the back yard we've wanted to hit the ball in the air. Well, here are my conclusions. As I stated before, when we're young, the ball comes in from high to low, so our swings go up to meet it. Well, that's kid stuff and it's over. The ball comes in on a line and that's just how our swings should be. Second, I guess we liked hitting the ball over a lot of ground, maybe to show what he-men we were. If we're mature hitters, that one should be over with, too. Third, the touchdown pass, the slam dunk, and the home run are big temptations in sports. How big? Hitters consistently rehearse swinging down in the on-deck circle because they know the merits of the top hand and level cut. Then they go into the heat of battle and lose their proper thinking. I tell you, try to hit that home run with an uppercut every time and you'll end up in a softball league.

Key: S = Strike
　　　 O = Out
　　　 P = Productive
　　　 PP = Potentially
　　　　　　 Productive

BALL TRAJECTORY vs. PRODUCTIVITY

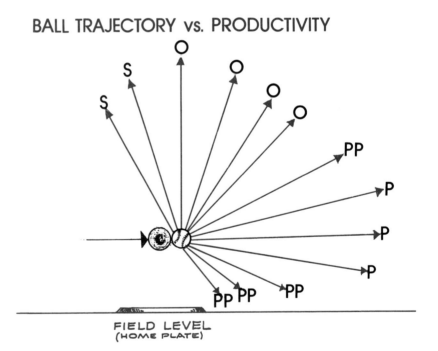

FIELD LEVEL
(HOME PLATE)

Why ground balls? Because productive hitting depends on how effective your "mis-hits" are. Take it from me, much less than 50 percent of your swings will connect on less than square contact. Say you're a good hitter and 25 percent of your swings are line drives. That leaves 75 percent as missed swings, foul balls, fly balls, and grounders. To your average and team production, a hundred ground balls would be much more effective than a hundred fly balls because 90 percent of the fly balls come to nothing. But only about 60 percent of ground balls are useless. A good percentage of them find holes and get you on base. Others cause errors and move up runners. Your bat coming down through the strike zone from high to level is what produces the ground balls and line drives. We don't have to worry about the balls we hit on the nose. Productive hitting comes from what we get on our miss-hit balls.

Here are just a few of the hitters who subscribe to this theory:

Aaron	Dick Allen	Winfield
Clemente	Puckett	Ripken
Al Oliver	Dave Parker	Sandberg

Coming from a home run hitter, this philosophy may surprise you. But take a look, the players I have named are sluggers, not banjo hitters.

Think about it. No-hitters are made up of roll-over weak ground balls, pop-ups, and fly balls. A game has twenty-seven outs. Twenty-seven fly balls and the game is usually over. Twenty-seven ground balls and you're in the seventh inning with a few runs.

This is why you've heard me emphasize over and over again the value of the top hand—to level out the swing and "crack the whip." If I was front arm extension oriented, I would not have been effective against the right-handed pitcher and would have hit about 250 less home runs. Front arm extension will get you an uppercut and the whip won't crack. You won't be as effective against the like-hander, the high strike, or hard throwers. If I don't crack the whip with the top hand, Gooden throws the ball by me. Nobody alive can hit these kinds of fast balls with a long loop in their swings. At best they will be hit in the air. *The top hand push/swing shortens and finishes the stroke.*

Now, look just a bit higher in the strike zone by programming your level swing mechanics, and a few of your line drives will get the trajectory and back spin to go out of the park. That's how I did it. Ditto Sandberg, Winfield, Allen, Ripken and the rest. Most of Aaron's home runs were deep line drives, not towering fly balls.

I believe that hitting .400 is possible again in the major leagues, given the right kind of hitter with the right kind of foundation and an injury-free season. To do it, in every block of ten at-bats his goal should be: 4+ line drives, 4+ ground balls, 2- fly balls.

3. Final Conscious Pre-swing Thought

The final pre-swing thought is the last "conscious" thought you have before your body reacts naturally to the pitch. It becomes your batting "theme." Since you can control this thought, why not think something that will effect your swing in a positive way? If your final thought is "home run" you're dead. It killed me, a home run hitter, plenty of times. Find a thought that you can use consistently, one that helps you produce a good swing in any situation—nobody on base in the first inning or bases loaded in the ninth. Believe and trust in this thought.

From 1985-1989 my final pre-swing thought became "swing down and up the middle." I visualized a line drive at the pitcher's knees. This pre-swing thinking directly influenced my mechanics in a positive way. This swing-thought idea translates good thoughts into good swings. More times than I can remember I thought "down and up the middle" and the ball ended up in the gap or in the seats with plenty of backspin.

Remember, under pressure your swing action is the result of your final conscious pre-swing thinking. Make yours productive and consistent. Here are some possible pre-swing thoughts I used from time to time to shore up immediate problems: "line drive to right center" (lefty would say left center), "keep the head down", "quick hands", "stay on top," "Clemente."

4. Visual Reminders

Hitting may be the strongest test of a hitter's thinking in sports. There is a lot going on inside the batter's box. To be effective, "untentative," your mind will have to be clear once you look the pitcher in the eyes, so your preparation has to take place before the games. Much of hitting is reminding yourself of key, correct principles, forgetting them, and bringing yourself back to them. Your coach will be a help, but you'll also have to be your own coach. Because I wanted my mind clear in the batter's box, other than my final conscious thought, I did a lot of my own "coaching" starting in the locker room. The last ten years of my career I made a list of my own ten hitting rules:

1. Relaxation	6. Mid-line movement
2. Rhythm	7. Steady head
3. Launch position	8. Observation
4. Hips	9. Strategy
5. Level swing plane	10. Final pre-swing thought

In this list you'll find the answer to any problem in hitting. I wrote these rules on a piece of paper and read it before and sometimes after games. I got to where I could pick out my own trouble spot to work on. You'd be surprised how it could explain a bad night at the plate and give me something to work on the next day.

THE TOTAL EFFORT

Everybody, every developing player, needs a model, someone he can follow, someone he can pattern himself after. I told you who my hitting models were—Aaron, Allen, and Clemente. They were fine men and great models to pattern my hitting after. Yet there was another player I tried to pattern my entire career after, someone I never knew. Lou Gehrig was my idol as a person and a player, and still is. *Pride of the Yankees* starring Gary Cooper was my favorite movie. To me, Gehrig most symbolized what a real ballplayer is. Read about him, check the Baseball Encyclopedia. If you want to further your career, imitate Lou Gehrig. He did as much on the field as anybody, in less time. Not only was he there everyday, he put the team first in every case. A team man is an RBI man, and Lou was the best RBI man of all time. He hit behind Ruth all those years and let him take most of the headlines. Gehrig was content to do his job every day as a team man with a professional approach, and it was never duplicated or corrupted.

Lou Gehrig.

I was fortunate to play in three World Series', be on a World Championship team, to win several home run and RBI titles, three Most Valuable Player awards, among other honors. Not many people know this, but the award I covet the most is the Lou Gehrig Award I was given in 1986. To me, Gehrig was the ultimate player, and to be given an award in his name went beyond the things I did on the field.

Perhaps as a small tribute, I would like to portray the Iron Horse the way that I imagine he was. This portrayal is sketched from the bits and pieces I learned about Lou along the trail, and from the image I held of him as I was coming along. If I can do this with some accuracy, and I believe I can, perhaps the Iron Horse will be able to lead you on as he did me.

Abraham Lincoln once said, "I will study and prepare myself, for someday I know my chance will come." Lou Gehrig thought along these same lines and prepared himself in many ways. He had strengthened himself through resistance (weight) training and various conditioning methods of his day. He had not built himself up to the point of winning body building trophies; this was neither necessary nor practical, and he knew it would be disadvantageous in terms of added weight. His time was better spent on the field, fine tuning his baseball skills. He had conditioned his whole body, and concentrated maximum buildup only in the arms, legs, and hands.

Gehrig had also conditioned his mind. He told himself early on that nothing short of the Lord would stop him from being a big league ballplayer. He knew there would be obstacles. He steeled his mind to move them, use them, or conquer them all. He believed that if he was given the gifts, then he was also given a way.

His diet was constructed to give him every advantage. He regarded his "fuel" with utmost care. He ate good food, not junk food—plenty of fruit, vegetables, carbohydrates, protein, and whole grains. Alcohol, popular in his day among other sluggers, was eliminated. In fact, drugs and alcohol were so far gone from his realm that they weren't even an issue. The same can be said for any other lure or addiction which would cause an unbalanced state and result in spiritual drain. He had the wisdom to know that when the good Lord grants you a special opportunity, it's worth sacrificing the things which are in conflict with that opportunity.

Gehrig believed that the team was more important than any individual. To Lou, the team effort came first. He encouraged his teammates at all times, and took care to help them both on and off the field. A credo he lived by was, "God first, the other fellow (and teammates) second, I am third." Nor did he forget about home, family, personal commitments and problems. He tended to these with the care they needed.

Lou Gehrig arrived at the ballpark physically and mentally prepared. For efficiency, and to avoid physical injury, he thoroughly loosened his body in preparation for pre-game practice and maintained his condition with dry cuts and sprints. His batting practice was purposeful; he didn't waste time trying to see how far he could hit the ball. This was the time to rehearse correct movement and work on trouble spots. Work at his position was undertaken the same way.

By the time he had secured his footing in the batter's box, Lou had a plan from the available information at hand. He was engaged in the process of judging his opponent and his skills, realizing that the pitcher is formidable and has a plan of his own. As the game progressed, he assembled clues from what the pitcher showed him, consulted teammates and passed on what he knew, and he was ready to adjust to new information. He operated self-sufficiently with the goal of contributing to team victory. Gehrig was the ultimate Combination Hitter. To be as good as he was, he combined every positive aspect of hitting into a unified whole—power and average, rotation and weight shift, percentages and guessing, observable clues and knowledge, fear and faith, balance and rhythm, hands and hips, power and grace, strength and humility, coaching and his own intuition.

At the game's conclusion Lou gathered his equipment, showered, and win or lose, completed the day by preparing his body for tomorrow's game. If the writers paid more attention to Ruth or Lazzeri or anyone else, he didn't let it bother him. Gehrig was playing with higher goals in mind, like doing the most with his gifts of skill and helping his team to the top. In this pursuit, he was already preparing for tomorrow's game. This included, in addition to nourishment and rest, an awareness of today's mistakes and successes. Rather than being done punitively, his game reflection was done as a way of feedback for improvement. He did this with belief in his skills, belief that he was operating in harmony with God's gifts, and with the conviction that his contributions to the world around him consisted of the contribution he made to both the game and the people involved with it.

To me, this was who Lou Gehrig was. And from the coaches and people who knew him that I have heard, I believe I am quite accurate. This is why I'm proud of my Gehrig award.

Problem Solving

PROBLEM: I'm a right-handed hitter playing high school baseball. I've hit clean up on about every team I've played on. I can hit for distance in batting practice. In the games I strike out a lot and have trouble with curve balls. What should I do?

SOLUTION: If you're hitting for distance in batting practice you're probably pulling the ball, ramming every delivery into the pull field, making contact way out in front of the plate, which is easy in batting practice but too tough in a game. Your trouble with breaking pitches would confirm this.

First, you've got to get more contact. Play a lot of pepper and get the idea of square, center field contact, more over the plate instead of in front of it. Back off the plate and get the feel of waiting a bit longer on the pitch and pushing with your hands. This will allow you to wait longer on the ball. Employ weight shift and take some of the weight over your front leg, rather than severely rotating against it. Level out your bat and make sure your stride is straight ahead, with the front foot landing close to parallel to the front edge of home plate.

Some hitters shift their weight forward too quickly, getting themselves out in front before the breaking ball arrives. If you find yourself getting out too quickly, Williams' knee turn will delay your stride. Also, know the fast ball counts. In these counts, you can go for the fences, the center field fence that is.

You might listen closely to some words from **Harry Walker:** "Most hitters, at least 75 percent of them, would be better off if they hit the ball more over the plate, straight away. When a hitter goes into a slump, nine out of ten times he's trying to hit the ball too far out in front of the plate. To get out of the slump shorten the stride, wait a little longer, hit the ball further back and hit it straight away."

Which sounds a lot like pepper.

PROBLEM: I love the game but I'm not having much luck at the plate. I'm small for my age but can run like the wind. Any ideas?

SOLUTION: Plenty. Don't fret if you're small; this game is for people of all sizes. Speed can make a hitter. Look at Ozzie Smith. Get batting left-handed today; the sooner switch hitting is begun the better chance it will take. Get on the left side of the plate and into a weight shift hitting style, which will help your strength and speed. Work on bunting while you're picking it up. Lots of pepper—you want square contact. Keep your hopes alive. With speed and weight shift, you've got a good chance.

PROBLEM: I'm a left-handed hitter and have trouble with left-handed pitching. What do I do?

SOLUTION: Two immediate solutions. Learn to drag bunt to the first base side and use it if no runner is on first. If somebody is on, try the third baseman, but keep it away from the pitcher. If you're thrown out, you still help the cause by moving the runner up. Next, look only for the fast ball up to two strikes with a hit-and-run attitude. Swing at the first fast ball you see. While you're doing these, work on keeping your weight back (uncommitted) with a knee turn, and use some hip rotation by bracing against a slightly angled front leg. You'll need tee work for this. Last, get a little more top hand into your swing. This will quicken your bat so you'll have more time to judge the curve.

PROBLEM: I have no confidence. I'm a lousy hitter. Sometimes I dread my turn at bat. What do I do?

SOLUTION: Don't despair. Outs are the best lessons you'll ever get, and it sounds like you're getting plenty. Analyze them. The pitcher is the best teacher you will ever have. Tip your cap to him, he's showing you what is wrong. Your statement, "I'm just a lousy hitter" shows that you are under the spell of bad thinking and fearful thought patterns. Have you ever gotten a hit? If so, something worked. For starters, read the section on Self Talk and practice it today. If you remain negative, you'll have to get out of the game. Playing negative is bad for the spirit and no fun. Change your thinking and it will become fun. Accept your failures as lessons and learn from them. Each time you put the ball in play, pat yourself on the back and build on it.

PROBLEM: The inside pitch eats me alive. What should I do?

SOLUTION: Few players hit a good inside fast ball consistently, and those that do have trouble with breaking balls. A hitter with a weakness inside usually hits the ball away effectively. If that is you, learn to take the inside pitch up to two strikes. Pitchers can't put it there consistently enough to get a batter out at will. If you can take this one and hit the rest, you can do more than most hitters.

Every hitter has some pitch he hits less effectively than others. Sometimes it is breaking balls, or inside pitches, or outside pitches. If you make an adjustment, you'll open up a weakness somewhere else. One of the best things the hitter can do is take the pitches he doesn't hit well, up to two strikes. He'll discover that the balls begin racking up, the count turns to his favor, and now he gets his pitch.

PROBLEM: How can I get my hitters to have more discipline at the plate?

SOLUTION: Discipline comes from taking full cuts with rhythm, balance, timing, and a healthy follow through at pitches *which are strikes*. Undisciplined swings happen when one or more of these is absent. If the hitter cannot execute with these, he shouldn't swing. In other words, when his timing is off, he should take the pitch unless he has two strikes.

Have your hitters practice full, ideal cuts in a group. It's a great practice starter. After cals or stretching, have all your hitters grab a bat and practice full cuts for just five minutes a day. Emphasize that these are the swings you want them to take at home plate. As a variation, have them take faulty cuts without timing, or at bad pitch areas, so they can feel the difference. When they get the feel of good cuts versus bad ones, they will take full cuts or none at all. It will take plenty of attention on your part.

PROBLEM: Whenever I swing, my front shoulder flies up and I uppercut everything. What will stop this?

SOLUTION: Something is not allowing your bat to get into the contact zone on time. Nine times out of ten this is because the hitter is not using his hands properly or he has no pre-swing movement. He's not whipping the bat with his hands. Instead of using hand strength to start the bat he uses the whole front side of his body, particularly the front shoulder, to pull the bat into the contact zone.

He'll typically rear up the front shoulder in a last ditch effort to get the bat on the ball. The hands are the *governor* of the baseball stroke, if they are working correctly. The hips and torso fall in line with the bat. Good hand work dictates good hip and leg work.

This hitter should practice dry swings, whipping the bat with his hands only. He'll get the feel of power in his hands. Also, he'll need some work on level body segment rotation. As he is emphasizing his hands in the dry cuts and tee work, he must make sure his hips and shoulders are rotating on level planes. He should be working with a flat bat angle.

Uppercutters often hit off their back legs, which have a tendency to collapse. The hitter should make sure he is hitting

146

with his weight against the front leg, not over the back leg. Also, in attacking the problem, whip yourself with words from **Charlie Lau:** "Uppercutting puts you in a weak position at the moment of contact and thus robs you of your natural power."

PROBLEM: What can be done about the hitter who pulls his head?

SOLUTION: Chances are this player is trying to pull the ball. Or, he may be over emphasizing his front side—the front arm and shoulder—in pulling the bat around. Convince him to stop trying to pull the ball and get him to use his hands. The direction of his hands, their force, should be into the strike zone *from the side,* not pulling it from back to front and around. Also, borrow from Lau. Have the hitter release his top hand after contact is made and make him *stare* at the contact by keeping his head down.

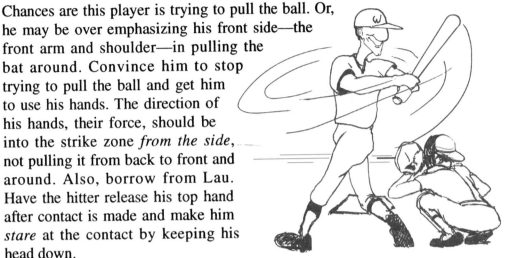

QUESTION: Doesn't rolling over the wrists produce a ground ball?

ANSWER: No. Contact is never made with the pitch after the top hand has extended forward all the way, which happens in the "one o'clock" area of the swing (eleven o'clock left-handed time). An illustrative analogy would be the person chopping down a tree with an axe. Both hands are on the axe when contact is made; they do not roll over. If they did, the lumberjack would be too damn far away from the tree to be chopping it. Making contact as the wrists roll over indicates massive timing problems. It is hard to imagine a hitter doing this unless he is completely fooled.

QUESTION: Can a batter swing level while emphasizing his top hand? It seems to me like he would be uppercutting.

ANSWER: The top hand has nothing to do with uppercutting. Top hand simply adds thrust, the bottom hand helps guide direction. A number of hitters hit with a chop, a stroke with a downward angle. This downward chop is characterized by a high bat angle and dominated by the top hand also.

QUESTION: I've heard that the hitter should finish high in his swing. True?

ANSWER: Lau wants this to insure front arm extension. However, if you use top hand action your stroke should finish the plane of your swing. If you've taken a hack at a low pitch, your finish would be high, on a high pitch, low, provided you have level shoulder rotation. Game photos show Gehrig finishing low plenty of times. So did I. Mantle, McCovey, and Musial, too. Finishing low and short was a key for me because it meant I was using my hands, particularly my top hand, correctly, I had level shoulder rotation, and I had a level stroke. I think finishing high is the opposite of all these. A hitter might twist the bat upward with his wrists in follow-through, like Ruth did, but this is when the plane of the swing is finished. You'll finish high only if you want top spin line drives. I didn't. And finishing high can be an awkward place from which to drop the bat when racing to first base. Finishing low and short was a key for me because it meant I was using my hands, particularly my top hand, correctly, I had level shoulder rotation, and I had a level swing.

Roger Maris in low finish.

Harry Walker: "You finish high on the low pitch, and level off the finish on the high ball. You don't want to finish high on the high pitch."

PROBLEM: I am stiff when I hit. I don't seem to have any rhythm.

SOLUTION: Remember Charlie Lau's words, "You've got to go back in order to go forward," and Williams' twitch or hitch of the bat to get it started. Practice them. You need movement. Also, pick up a heavier bat and take dry cuts. They will force you to do these things.

Old Wives' Tales

A hitch is a hitting fault.

Don't buy it. That and putting your foot in the bucket can be valuable momentum-gaining devices, so long as the bucket is on line with the pitcher.

Shortening your stride will give you quickness.

It also robs you of a timing device and valuable weight shift. Shorten your stride and cut down your swing enough, you'll be playing pepper with the pitcher.

A hitter should never get jammed.

If he's not getting jammed occasionally, he's not anticipating the percentage pitch. Fighting off an inside fast ball by getting jammed is good hitting. So is a broken bat single, and a soft base hit to the opposite field. **Al Kaline:** "If a hitter isn't getting jammed from time to time, he's not waiting on the ball. He's pulling out his front side."

Good hitters don't guess.

Good hitters are good because they look for certain pitches in certain situations. When they are right they powder the pitch. And they're right more often than they're wrong. When they're wrong they take the pitch or, with two strikes, their mechanics adjust to help them out of a jam.

The front arm is the most important arm in hitting.

Both arms are important. Basically, the front arm provides direction, the rear arm strength. Both are vital.

Great hitters are born, not made.

All hitters are born. Some make themselves great.

Even the best hitters fail seven times out of ten.

Outs cannot be considered failures if you get information out of them which lead to your next success. Good hitters fail once, twice out of ten. The rest are hits and lessons.

Charlie Lau and Ted Williams are the best hitting instructors of all time.

Maybe. But every pitcher is right up there with them. They tell you unequivocally when you are wrong.

Going for home runs every time up is not good hitting.

It can be, if the hitter knows how, has the ability to hit them, knows how to get good counts and learns the pitchers. If he doesn't, he'll bury himself.

The knuckles should line up in the grip.

Knuckles, shmuckles.

A split grip gives more bat control.

True, but at the expense of power. Any gap at all between the hands results in a lessening of power because the wrist action is diminished.

The golf swing is the same as the baseball swing.

Double false. They can be compared, but only to illustrate the differences. Hitting a golf ball and hitting a baseball have too many different goals, implements, variables, time, and purposes, to be close kin. Further, the plane of the golf swing is roughly 90 degrees from that of the baseball stroke and so are most of the mechanics. Only one involves an opponent. The goal of one is accuracy, the other's goal is speed and quickness. A golfer has the luxury of time, the hitter has no such luxury. The golfer could not possibly complete his swing in the brief time it takes a pitch to arrive in the catcher's mitt. Therefore, the baseball swing requires a vital break from golf principles.

Pitchers' Tips

It may seem that in this section we are aiding and abetting the enemy. On the contrary. Under the assumption that the pitcher is the hitter's ultimate teacher, and he is, this section is meant to aid him in that task. Further, hitters should be quick in learning their weaknesses and the solutions to them faster than the pitcher. The hitter who doesn't, or won't, needs further encouragement. Besides, we've given away enough pitchers' tricks, and the game must remain in balance. Not only that, I'm sure there are a couple hitters out there who will end up their careers as pitchers.

When you face a hitter in a deep crouch at the knees, delay. Keep him in this position as long as you can. It will build up lactic acid in his muscles and drive him batty. When he realizes what you are doing, you've got him.

Six things a pitcher must master with his pitching: In, out, fast, slow, up, and down.

Use "elevation." When you've kept the ball low on a hitter three or four times in a row <u>and you've got a couple of strikes on him,</u> try a high strike. Hitters' eyes and mechanics can get stuck on location.

A hitter can look for a certain pitch, but never *velocity*. If he is leaning on a certain pitch he has seen before, and you have to give it to him, speed it up or slow it down from that which he has seen.

Pitch switch hitters low to the right side, high from the left side. It has to do with arm dominance.

Pitch weight shift hitters high, top hand dominant hitters low.

Nick the high inside corner with belt high, hard sliders to the opposite-handed hitter. It is next to impossible to hit well. If it is hit well, the angle makes it a foul ball. If not, you've got a good shot at a broken bat. Make sure you keep it up; low ones can be hit hard on the ground.

Generally, the farther you keep the ball away from the eyes of the like-handed hitter, the better.

Change-ups are doubly effective on the opposite-handed hitter. This has to do with his angle of vision to your release point.

Weak hitters are poor on inside sliders. Strong hitters murder them.

Look (don't glare) the hitter in the eye when he steps into the box. Noncompetitors will do a private retreat. Glaring will spur the competitor.

When you've lost a couple of feet off your fast ball late in the game, lose a couple more.

Challenge weak hitters, respect strong ones.

To a hitter who hit a home run off you on his last trip, challenge him on the first pitch. After that, pitch.

Don't bother setting up weak or strong hitters. Go right at their weaknesses. Set up the middle ground hitters.

Pitch to a weakness until the hitter makes an adjustment at the plate. Then go the opposite way.

Hands low, pitch high. Hands high, pitch low. Hands in, pitch in (but be ready to change.) Hands out, pitch out.

Weight shift, aim in. Rotation, aim out. Uppercutters, aim out.

Read foul balls to read a hitter's timing.

To the Hitter

So you want to be a hitter? What a wonderful pursuit you have chosen. I have never known a game besides baseball in which everyone connected wins so much. Your desire to excel in hitting puts you in the company of some great ones—Rose, Gehrig, Appling, Hornsby, Clemente, Ruth, Musial, Carew, Mantle, Mays, Foxx, Speaker, Williams—whose desires were the same as yours. To remain in their company you can not shirk your responsibilities. Are you prepared to accept a mountain of failure in return for painful lessons which will steer you in the right direction at a pace so slow you will be tempted to quit in exasperation? Are you willing to take the pain of so many defeats, and then review them again and again for lessons? Will your sense of humor and spirit survive to sustain you, or will it die along the way, making you a different person than the one who got you as far as you are. Can you keep your desire to learn and improve, even though many times it will appear that improvement does not come? Do you have the attitude required to let obstacles and restrictions penetrate only as far as what can be gained from examining them, and then shield yourself from them? These are questions you must ask yourself.

Unless you are a complete natural, which extremely few are, you will be required to devote hour upon hour of purposeful preparation and repetition. Can you practice a correct, full cut a thousand times, fifty times at a crack? Do you have the warrior inside you which will spur you on when all the others have gone home? You will be required to sift through a ton of knowledge and theories, and choose correctly between them. To do this, you'll need almost a spiritual connection, a gift of luck. When you do, will you have the where-with-all to structure the knowledge into your hitting make-up? When you are mired in slumps and the evil of discouragement, will you be able to survive on faith? The greatest struggle of all will be the one that takes place within your soul. It's a silent fight, not only waged in public view but also in darkness, in hotel rooms and locker rooms, on the way to and from the park, laying awake in bed, a battle between the forces of self-doubt and confidence, of fate and determination. After that you will be required to face scores of pitchers trying to make you fail. Will you be able to pick yourself up and stand when the battles are over?

If so, you will be a hitter. Maybe a high school hitter, maybe a college hitter, maybe a semi-pro. Maybe a pro, even a major leaguer. Regardless, if you give it your all and remain standing and still working, you'll be in the club. You'll know the kinship to Ruth, Waner, Sisler, and Aaron.

As a youngster, I "knew" a kinship to guys like Gus Bell, Frank Robinson, Gordy Coleman, Pete Rose, Tony Perez. By the age of fifteen I had been to Crosley Field where these guys played, then the home of the Cincinnati Reds. I dreamed of someday playing there with them. It was a long shot. As a high school freshman baseball player I was such a bad hitter that no summer team would have me. Before I was out of high school I had both knees operated on. Through high school I had never made an all-star team of any kind. I had to "walk on" through a try-out at Ohio University, about the only school interested in me. As a major league rookie I hit .196 and was ridiculed by everyone as one of the easiest guys in the league to strike out. But no one could ever finish me off. I had this "kinship" working, and was determined to succeed. I worked harder, tried different positions and stances, anything that might lead to something. They did and my rewards are well documented.

This book is an opportunity for me to share my secrets, what I found in my continuous search. It is my hope that this study will provide you with a solid foundation, that it might pioneer a new wave of productive hitters. You can be one of those hitters. You've learned from Williams, Lau, Hriniak, and other experts. And you've studied my approach, which combines a workable amount of each along with a knowledge of percentages and strategy. I've outlined strategy and planning, taken you deeply into the minds of some real experts, brought out their secrets and discoveries, even intruded into your thinking and your diet. I guess a good reason for this was to lighten your load and shorten your route, because it's a long haul to the big leagues. I know how every little bit counts when your dreams are at stake. Whether you make it all the way or stop at one of the mile markers along the path, give it all you've got. It's a wonderful road. I envy your journey.

Good luck.

Contributing Authorities

Rob Ellis

Co-Author

Rob Ellis played professional baseball for twelve seasons, including parts of four seasons in the major leagues with the Milwaukee Brewers. He has coached professionally with the San Francisco Giants and Chicago Cubs, and at his alma mater, Michigan State University where he was College Player of the Year in 1971. He is the author of three hitting videos, two books—*The Outfielder,* and *Michigan State Baseball: A Concerned Look,* and numerous magazine articles.

Contributing Specialists

Ben Hines, Los Angeles Dodgers Hitting Instructor. Hines is the only major league hitting coach to have mastered the skills of hitting at both the collegiate and professional levels. Ben coached at the University of LaVerne and Arizona State prior to joining the Dodgers. He is an innovator who is an authority on arm and hand action of the swing.

Ben Hines

Frank Howard, New York Yankees Hitting Coach. "Hondo" was the American Leagues' most feared hitter in the late 1960's when he was a prized pupil of Ted Williams. In 1968 through 1970 Howard had 44, 48, and 44 home run seasons. Having belted 382 home runs in his career, the huge slugger for the Los Angeles Dodgers, Washington Senators, Texas Rangers, and the Detroit Tigers was known for his tape measure blasts. Today he is an authority on the Williams theory and overall hitting movement.

Frank Howard

155

Walt Hriniak

Walt Hriniak, Chicago White Sox Hitting Coach. Hriniak is known as the leading authority of the Lau Weight Shift and offensive baseball. Like Lau, a left-handed hitting catcher in his playing days, Hriniak has developed more weight shift hitters at the major league level than any hitting coach. He is a disciplinarian known for improving the team batting averages wherever he has coached.

Clarence Jones, Atlanta Braves Hitting Instructor. Jones, a former major league outfielder and first baseman, is given credit for cultivating the offensive development of the 1991 National League champion Atlanta Braves.

Al Kaline

Al Kaline, First Ballot Hall of Fame outfielder of the Detroit Tigers. Kaline, a model hitter and all-around player for 22 major league seasons with the Tigers, is a career .297 hitter with 3007 hits and 399 home runs. Al was a master technician at the plate who never played in the minor leagues. He won the American League batting title at age twenty with a .340 average.

Frank Robinson

Frank Robinson, First Ballot Hall of Fame outfielder. Frank is one of the all-time greats of the game. He is fourth in major league career home runs with 586. A leader on every team he played on—the Reds, Dodgers, Orioles, Angels and Indians—his career average spanning 21 seasons is .294. A fierce competitor who managed three major league clubs, Frank is considered a master in all phases of hitting.

Harry "The Hat" Walker, former major league manager and 1947 National League batting champion (.363). Harry Walker was the first hitting instructor to construct a unified hitting system. Walker taught major league hitters for 40 years. One of the first weight shift instructors, Walker is credited with the development of National League batting champion Matty Alou. He managed three National League teams and played in three World Series.

Harry "The Hat" Walker

Bob Watson, former hitting instructor with the Atlanta Braves and Houston Astros. "Bull" Watson hit .295 in 19 major league seasons, during which he was one of the most consistent hitters in the game.

Billy Williams, Hall of Fame outfielder and hitting coach for the Chicago Cubs. Billy, a perennial triple crown threat, was known as one of the most consistent and durable men ever to play the game. He hit .290 in 18 seasons with 426 home runs. During his playing days Williams was known for his top hand action in his hitting style. Billy is considered an authority in all phases of hitting.

Bob Watson

Richie Zisk, Minor League hitting instructor, Chicago Cubs. Richie played thirteen seasons with the Pittsburgh Pirates, Chicago White Sox, Texas Rangers, and Seattle Mariners. He combined average with power to hit 207 home runs and averaged .287 over his career. One of only four players to have hit a home run in the centerfield bleachers at Comisky Park.

Richie Zisk

Mike Schmidt's Career Record

Year	Club	Avg.	G	AB	R	H	2b	3b	HR	RBI	BB	SO
1971	Reading	.211	74	237	27	50	7	1	8	31	27	66
1972	Eugene	.291	131	436	80	127	23	6	26	91	87	145
	Phillies	.206	13	34	2	7	0	0	1	3	5	15
1973	Phillies	.196	132	367	43	72	11	0	18	52	62	136
1974	Phillies	.282	162	568	108	160	28	7	36	116	106	138
1975	Phillies	.249	158	562	93	140	34	3	38	95	101	180
1976	Phillies	.262	160	584	112	153	31	4	38	107	100	149
1977	Phillies	.274	154	544	114	149	27	11	38	101	104	122
1978	Phillies	.251	145	513	93	129	27	2	21	78	91	103
1979	Phillies	.253	160	541	109	137	25	4	45	114	120	115
1980	Phillies	.286	150	548	104	157	25	8	48	121	89	119
1981	Phillies	.316	102	354	78	112	19	2	31	91	73	71
1982	Phillies	.280	148	514	108	144	26	3	35	87	107	131
1983	Phillies	.255	154	534	104	136	16	4	40	109	128	148
1984	Phillies	.277	151	528	93	146	26	3	36	106	92	116
1985	Phillies	.277	158	549	89	152	31	5	33	93	87	117
1986	Phillies	.290	160	552	97	160	29	1	37	119	89	84
1987	Phillies	.293	147	522	88	153	28	0	35	113	83	80
1988	Phillies	.249	108	390	52	97	21	2	12	62	49	42
1989	Phillies	.203	42	148	19	30	7	0	6	28	21	17
ML Totals		**.267**	**2404**	**8352**	**1506**	**2234**	**408**	**59**	**548**	**1595**	**1507**	**1883**

Schmidt's National and Major League Records

HITTING
(KEY: NL = National League; ML = Major League)

Most Years Leading League in Home Runs– 8 (NL)
Most Consecutive Years, 30 or More Homers– 9 (NL)
Most Years Leading League, RBI– 4 (NL)
Most Home Runs, Career, Third Baseman– 509 (ML)
Most Home Runs, Season, Third Baseman– 48 (ML)
Most RBI, Career, Third Baseman– 1595 (ML)
Most Home Runs, all 12 League Parks, Season 1979 (NL)
Most Home Runs Month of April– 11 (ML)
Most Home Runs Through April 30– 11 (ML)
Most Home Runs Through July 31– 36 (NL)
Most Home Runs Month of October– 4 (ML)
Most Home Runs, Game– 4 (ML)

—Continued on next page

Most Consecutive Home Runs, Game–
    4 (ML)
Most Consecutive Home Runs, Two
    Games– 4 (ML)
Most Home Runs, Two Straight Games,
    Hitting Homer Each Game– 5 (ML)
Most Home Runs, Three Straight Games,
    Homering in Each Game– 6 (ML)
Most Home Runs, Five Straight Games,
    Homering in Each Game– 7 (NL)
Most Total Bases, Extra-Inning Game–
    17 (ML)
Most Years Leading League in Extra Bases
    on Long Hits– 7 (NL)
Most Consecutive Years Leading League in
    Extra Bases on Long hits– 3 (NL)
Most Extra Bases on Long Hits Extra-
    inning
    Game– 12 (ML)
Most Consecutive Years Leading in Bases
    on Balls– 3 (NL)
Fewest Singles, Season, 150 or More
    Games– 63 (ML)

FIELDING (Third Basemen)

Most Years, League– 18 (NL)
Most Games, League– 2,212 (NL)
Most Assists, League– 5,025 (NL)
Most Total Chances, League– 6,922 (NL)
Most Double Plays, League– 456 (NL)
Most Gold Gloves– 10 (NL)
Most Assists, Season– 404 (NL)
Most Years Leading League in Assists– 7 (NL)
Most Years Leading League in Double Plays– 6 (NL)

RANKINGS ALL-TIME, MAJOR LEAGUES

Home Runs– 7th (548)
Multiple Home Run Games– Tie 10th (44)
Home Runs, One Stadium– 4th (265)
Extra Base Hits– 15th (1,015)
Total Bases– 26th (4,404)
Extra Bases On Long Hits– 15th (2,170)
RBI– 17th (1,595)
Sacrifice Flies– 4th (108)
Slugging Average– 15th (.527)
Walks– 13th (1,507)
Strikeouts– 3rd (1,883)
Games Played, Third Base– 3rd (2,211)

Other Hitting Sources

Other Hitting Aids available from McGriff & Bell Inc., 1579 Monroe Dr. N.E., Suite 134, Atlanta, Georgia, 30324, 1-800-642-0562:

The Mike Schmidt Study: Youth Version: Building A Hitting Foundation, Mike Schmidt and Rob Ellis. This book is intended for players 8 to 15 years old, their fathers and coaches. Pictures and illustrations throughout. Easy-to-follow teaching steps designed to teach a fundamentally sound baseball swing based on major league action. Drills, light explanations of fundamentals, introduction to mental strategy. ISBN 0-9634-6093-5 72 pages. $10.95.

Videos

(All three videos $69 plus $6 postage and handling.)

The Professional Hitter, Rob Ellis, 100 minutes. Explanation and demonstration of every pro hitting skill using college and professional players as examples. Mechanics, stroke adjustments, step-by-step progression. Highly acclaimed by college and professional authorities. $49.95.

Teaching Professional Skills, Rob Ellis, 60 minutes. Team and individual drills designed to acquire professional skills. Stance, mechanical execution, hitting philosophy, self-talk. Demonstrations throughout. $39.95.

Hitting Simplification, Rob Ellis, 45 minutes. Pro secrets and mental strategy used by major league players to simplify the hitting skill. Game examples and player demonstrations. Ground breaking instruction welcomed by coaches and players alike. A must for the serious player. $39.95.

Fiction

The Mendoza Line, Treavor Lake. The tale of a major league batting champion who falls to cocaine only to rise again. Light humor mixed with subtle tragedy. Mature readers. ISBN 0-9634-6094-3, paperback, $5.95.